More Charlotte Mason EDUCATION

A HOME SCHOOLING HOW-TO MANUAL

Catherine Levison

More Charlotte Mason EDUCATION

A HOME SCHOOLING HOW-TO MANUAL

Catherine Levison

CHAMPION PRESS, LTD.
BEVERLY HILLS

CHAMPION PRESS, LTD.
BEVERLY HILLS, CALIFORNIA
NEW EDITION
Copyright © 2000 Catherine Levison

Group discounts are available. For more information call (360) 576 9261.

Cataloging-in-Publication Data
    Levison, Catherine.
        More Charlotte Mason education: a home schooling
        how-to manual/Catherine Levison.—New ed.
        p. cm.
        Includes bibliographical references.
        LCCN: 99-74641
        ISBN: 1-891400-17-7
        1. Mason, Charlotte M. (Charlotte Maria), 1842-1923.
    2. Education—Philosophy. 3. Home schooling. 4. Education—Curricula.
    5. Christian education. I. Title.

    LB775.M359L48 1999   371.39

                                  96-228741

Also by Catherine Levison, *A Charlotte Mason Education*

10 9 8 7 6 5 4 3 2

Book and Cover Design by Kathy Campbell, Wildwood Studios.

Printed in Canada.

*T*his book is dedicated to all of your
Charlotte Mason days

Table of Contents

ONE

Charlotte Mason the person

The many people who personally knew Charlotte Mason loved her deeply and were able to describe her in vivid detail. Whether they met her early in her lifetime or near its end their impressions of her are very consistent. Young and old alike found her to be inspirational, humorous and humble.

Her love of children was so evident that it could not be ignored and was often viewed as her most profound attribute. This love formed into a deep concern that children would develop a lifetime love of learning. She based her philosophy on the Latin word for education, "educare" which means "to feed and nourish."

Although her methodology impacted the entire country of England she did not let it go to her head—she wanted her work to go on but not her name. Her friend Elsie Kitching wrote "Charlotte Mason lived to be eighty-one. She did not keep letters or diaries. 'I do not wish my life to be written, it is the work that matters: it will live.'"

Regardless of her humility she was well known throughout England. From the royal family on down, the entire country felt her influence. Sir Michael Sadler wrote, "She threw 'a shaft of light across the land.'" No doubt some of her national recognition was due to Mr. Household who was the County Secretary for Education in England when he became aware of Charlotte Mason's work in 1917. After receiving a pamphlet regarding her work he visited her in person for several days in 1919 at Scale How. (They had already corresponded by mail for years.) Essex Cholmondeley later wrote that Mr. Household was tireless in spreading interest about Charlotte's philosophies, and the results were that he was granted permission, beginning with five schools, to provide Charlotte Mason-type books to them. The interest grew to 50 schools with a total of 10,500 students benefiting from the method.

Remarkably, Charlotte Mason developed her educational insights as a young woman and even more astonishing is the fact that after decades of working with children and using her ideas with them she did not waver in her philosophy. Her friend Henrietta Franklin wrote, "Quite early she had taken as the text of her mission these words of Benjamin Whichcote, 'No sooner doth the truth . . . come into the soul's sights, but the soul knows her to be her first and old acquaintance.'" (*Netta*, p. 35)

Education was quite different in Charlotte Mason's day than we find it now. According to a World Wide Education Service (WES) pamphlet she lived in the era when "they practised reading, writing and arithmetic, sitting bolt upright on hard chairs (no slouching was allowed!) and writing on a piece of slate which could be wiped clean and used again. They were often given long lists to learn by heart, such as capital cities or dates from history or hard spellings. If they did not learn their work they were punished, sometimes by caning..."

We need to remember that much of what Charlotte Mason wrote about was in reaction to the above system and other educational theories of her day. Her material was written to a society much different than our own. In our day a small minority find Charlotte Mason's teachings to be "child centered" and they intend that as a negative comment. We need to think back to a callous society that cared very little about children and even less about what they had to say (if they were permitted to talk at all) to consider the severity of the situation that Mason observed. One of Charlotte's many biographers Jenny King wrote, "Charlotte Mason was probably the first educationalist to advocate visits to museums, galleries, concerts . . . [and the children] are free to relate their own impressions after the visit." We live in a different time with a much more permissive society—we can only guess about what kind of advice Charlotte Mason might have for us now.

Some of the Charlotte Mason home schooling parents have *not* lost sight of what era Charlotte was living—in fact they are *very* conscious of it. Many who follow her method seem to think of her a little differently than I do. While others have a mental image of a pristine woman, surrounded by lace and tea paraphernalia, I keep a quite different impression in my mind. I imagine a sturdy pair of muddied boots with some otherwise sensible clothing to equip her for the field. Her frequent walks across the English countryside in all kinds of weather are well documented. I'm sure she was every bit as feminine as the next lady, but I can visualize her casting off the bits of lace and other unnecessary fluff when it was time to head outdoors. My imaginings were somewhat proven true by this description of Charlotte's college, "The actual surroundings, the books, the pictures, the simple furniture and wild flowers for decorations were a revelation in themselves in those days when the world lived in a crowd of ancestral treasures or the unutterable hideousness of the Victorian age." (*Charlotte Mason College*, p. 17) Personally, I love antique furniture, books and houses, but the fact that Charlotte lived and wrote in another time is not the sole reason I'm interested in her teachings.

When Mason was eighteen years old she attended one of the only colleges set up for the training of teachers. They taught her that the performer (the child) was of more importance than the performance of the child. Matthew Arnold and John Ruskin's philosophies both promoted going beyond the three R's (reading, writing and arithmetic) and a combination of their views insisted that inclusion of literature, poetry, religion, art and nature were necessary. Obviously, these teachings made a lasting impression on her.

There was also a debate among the educationalists of the time. They were in flux about the goals of female education. Charlotte Mason found herself in a time when the very goal of feminine education was in question. Should the women be trained in "accomplishments" or should they have "sound learning?" Meanwhile the "contemporary medical opinion really thought that too much mental effort was dangerous to women." (*Charlotte Mason College,* p. 6–7) There is no doubt that she lived during an interesting time when many traditional concepts were being questioned. Evidently, some thought the girls should be given the same education as the boys, but many disagreed.

Amid all of the theories, experiments and debates Charlotte Mason made her determination: A liberal education for everybody was her answer. Of course she did not invent the Liberal Arts, she just wanted children to enjoy them more than the previous educators of her day. Her love for the children and the disadvantaged led her to some innovative ideas for her time. She gave both, the impoverished and the young, the benefit of the doubt and made the assumption that they were not below understanding literature and the fine arts. Most of us would agree with her now, but at the end of the 19th century that was a revolutionary way of thinking.

Charlotte was ill a great deal of her life and many who write about her find they must include their observations of her health. One of the most touching descriptions was written by Household. His account of their visit was published in both *In Memoriam of Charlotte M. Mason* and in *The Story of Charlotte Mason.* Even though she was ill he wrote that her face did not show any signs of weariness or pain and that she had quietly put those away from herself. He tells us, "Her face was full of light, of wide sympathy and understanding, of delicate humor and gentleness and love. When she talked with you she brought out the best that was in you, something that you did not know was there . . . she caught you up to her level, and for the time you stayed there; and you never quite fell back again." He went on to say, "In any difficulty she always saw the right way. With few words. Always perfectly chosen, yet coming naturally and without trace of effort, she said what you knew at once to be the right thing, though you had groped long and had not found it." And, "It is not yet the time to measure up her whole achievement. The full harvest is not yet. But there is enough to justify the confidence that posterity will see in her a great reformer, who led the children of the nation out of a barren wilderness into a rich inheritance . . . the children of many generations will thank God for Charlotte Mason and her work."

That certainly has come true. People are truly thankful when they see the benefits in their children and their ability to learn. One mother shared with me, "The complaining has almost come to a stop. They even say I don't work them as hard—but the funny thing is they are learning more." Another wrote, "We're having fun!" Parents and children across the world are still finding out how they can incorporate literature, nature and art appreciation to their joy and not merely because it's expected of them.

One of Charlotte's students wrote of her, "Somehow, in her presence, meanness and pettiness fell away, and one believed in and strove to reach the highest of which one was capable. And not only this—one learnt to believe in the goodness and joy of life. One felt that, at the back of all Miss Mason's teaching, was a philosophy of life based on an intense conviction of the personal relationship of every individual soul with God—a relationship that was the basis of all joy in living." (*In Memoriam of Charlotte M. Mason*, p. 77) Another testimony to the high esteem many held for her is also a mention of her relationship to God.

It is not possible to separate Charlotte Mason, the person, or her educational philosophies from Christianity. I have done extensive research on this matter and know it to be true, but I have also decided that the subject speaks for itself in her writings. Amid the ample proof of her personal faith is the knowledge that her two closest friends were of other faiths, one being Jewish and the other a Quaker. These friendships are further evidence of her magnanimity while it does not change the fact that Charlotte's Christianity is unquestionable.

Charlotte Mason was also a Sunday school teacher. Various churches and individuals today are employing these methods and finding them to be very satisfying for all involved. Imagine a Sunday school classroom without glitter, glue and pipe cleaners. Instead of busywork a sketchbook has been provided to each student with their names on the cover. Rather than calling it a nature notebook, refer to it as "God's Book of Creation" and sketch objects that God has indeed created. Include Bible selections referring to creation or nature, and hymns pertaining to nature. Imagine a room that uses the actual Bible and has the children narrate what the teacher has read—very effective, very reliable. Thirdly, the occasional use of masterpiece art that depicts the Bible scenes with elegance and accuracy easily takes the place of useless visual aids.

Charlotte died in her sleep and her funeral was described by one of her students. She wrote, "We went in procession, the children (of the practicing school) following most closely with flowers in their hands, the staff and college by twos, carrying the wreaths, winding slowly out of the gate and into the village. The wind and the rain blew coldly up from the lake, and the people came out to their doors, the men with their hats off and the women looking after us as we turned towards the church. We laid flowers beside the grave and passed one by one. It looked so small to be the resting place of that great spirit." (*Charlotte Mason College*, p. 17)

An entire book is dedicated to remembrances such as this. Charlotte Mason was greatly loved and her parting was deeply felt by her friends and acquaintances. Their reflections were published in the book, *In Memoriam of Charlotte M. Mason,* and if you truly want to understand her as a person, you'll want to request a copy through interlibrary loan.

A friend of mine resides in England and has visited Charlotte's grave. She is buried in St Mary's Parish Church, Ambleside and the gravestone reads:

> "In loving memory of Charlotte Maria Shaw Mason, Born Jan 1 1842, died Jan 16 1923, Thine eyes shall see the King in His beauty. Founder of the Parents National Educational Union, The Parents Union School and The House of Education. She devoted her life to the work of education, believing that children are dear to our heavenly Father, and that they are a precious national possession. Education is an atmosphere, a discipline, a life. I am, I can, I ought, I will. For the children's sake."

As Household commented, Charlotte Mason brings you up to her level. Like many I'm grateful to have found out about her teachings and I think you'll agree it's truly phenomenal that such a long time after one woman's death we find that she is still able to bring a whole generation up to her level.

TWO

An Overview
of the Charlotte Mason Method

Charlotte Mason developed an educational philosophy that entails countless techniques and ideals. It's not uncommon for educators to develop educational philosophies and goals, however, the majority will change and adapt them as they gain experience. Charlotte Mason, however, did not alter her philosophy at any point of her life.

She wrote prolifically about her method and practiced it with children through classroom situations and correspondence-styled home schools. Decade after decade she witnessed children being educated with her philosophy and saw that it really worked.

Of all the ideals from a Charlotte Mason education one could choose as the most representative, I believe it is this: We are to help the child develop a love for learning. Goals, like this one, are significant because they have a way of permeating every facet of education.

Ideas impact people in different ways. Sometimes when there is relatively little input or influence upon the new home schooler their first instinct is to duplicate "school at home." Most people will admit to following that example unless another philosophy was presented to them first. Often classroom teaching is what they grew up with and that's what they set out to accomplish—it becomes their goal. I can tell you from personal experience that attempting to run a rigid replica of a classroom in a home environment does not last long.

Another example of how goals influence our choices comes from my first year. When I was new to home schooling I only had one goal—I wanted to have my children at grade level. That goal permeated every choice I made and every product I purchased. Eventually, I came to see that home schooling was probably a permanent situation in my life and only when I realized my children were going to be in my care for all thirteen school years did a significant change occur.

About that same time the philosophies of Charlotte Mason came into my life and had a profound impact on my home schooling, but it certainly was not an overnight sensation. First, I grappled with what the method itself entailed and inevitably I had to learn how to apply it in a way that would work for me and my children.

The love for learning became the goal for my home and no other goal has affected us as profoundly. Knowing that children can graduate from school while still loving the learning process itself, and also feel confident in their abilities, seemed like a far cry from the education I had received. Many people in my generation left school feeling scholastically inadequate, even those who had high grade point averages.

The primary strategy for developing the love of learning is to not kill the love in the first place. If you're asking yourself, "Who would ever do that?" think back over your purchases. Frequently, home schoolers buy a high priced educational product that later we find the children hate. One clear indication is if every time you pull a certain product out everyone in the room swoons with objections and even *you* can't stand the sight of it—that is killing the love for learning. Why do you keep pulling it out? Because it was expensive and you can't bear the thought of putting it aside. Two goals are at odds with each other in that scenario. You want "to get your money's worth" but ultimately the best choice is to set your mind on a more lasting goal and find a more interesting way to present the same teaching.

Love for learning does not entail a party atmosphere in your school. We do not surround our children with circus clowns, balloons and pony rides to achieve our goal. Charlotte Mason did not advocate the avoidance of the unattractive subjects. If she had, we would have been left to assume that the love for learning should take precedence over subjects the children didn't care for. She personally thought grammar was one of the unattractive subjects. Instead of disregarding it, she wrote a grammar book for her students to use.

The key is to present the most interesting books and other materials we can possibly find for our children. Charlotte was a big believer in challenging the children intellectually. Rather than "dumbing down" the next generation and priding ourselves on creating a love of learning by easing their load, we want to assume that their intelligence is equivalent to our own. In Charlotte's day the child was not given the benefit of the doubt. She wrote, "Hard things are said of children, that they have 'no brains' a low order of intellect,' . . ." (Vol. 6, p. 25) The I. Q. test of today reveals the truth of her assumption that children are as intelligent as adults. Ordinarily, I. Q. results do not vary throughout a lifetime, a person will receive approximately the same score regardless of how many times they are tested. (Special needs children are an exception—more about this later in this chapter.) It is helpful for educators to view children this way. In fact Charlotte asked, "Does the teacher . . . perceive that intellect is enthroned before him in every child, however dull and inattentive may be his outer show?" (Vol. 6, p. 50) I'm thankful for that statement because I have children who occasionally display a "dull and inattentive" look. I practice what Charlotte taught and I give them the benefit of the doubt. This is especially helpful with the expressionless face common with teenagers. I think you know the look I'm referring to.

Assuming a higher intelligence and avoiding boring materials leads to more than a love of learning. You'll find children are on the road to "self education." According to Charlotte this happy state is supposed to be an "enormous relief to teachers" and I couldn't agree more.

Classroom teaching sometimes hinders this advancement by relying on what Charlotte would call, "torrents of talk, in tedious repetition" with the responsibility of learning on the wrong shoulders. She wrote, "All school work should be conducted in such a manner that children are aware of the responsibility of learning; it is their business to know that which has been taught. To this end the subject matter should not be repeated . . . these repeated aids result in our being persons of wandering attention and feeble memory. To allow repetition of a lesson is to shift the responsibility for it from the shoulders of the pupil to those of the teacher who says, in effect,—'I'll see that you know it,' so his pupils make no effort of attention." (Vol. 6, p. 74) That is exactly what parents and teachers are guilty of—trying too hard to ensure that the child knows the material we are trying to teach him.

To bring about self education we need to use direct contact. By that, I mean, we bring the best literature, art, music, poetry, etc. directly to the child as early in life as possible. We provide an education by the humanities while allowing the child's mind to act upon the material on its own, without interference. Two things help with this immensely. Becoming choosy about reading material and using narration in school.

Choosing quality reading material involves avoiding children's books that are dumbed down or written to them as though they are on a lower level intellectually. We can solve this problem in several ways. One way is to choose books that are written *to* children not *down* to them. Two authors who are good examples are Beatrix Potter and A. A. Milne. Both are gifted authors and have delighted generations of children, however, neither of them insults their intelligence.

Another great idea is to read adult level books to children such as *Oliver Twist* by Charles Dickens. Not too many six or seven year olds are capable of reading that book unassisted. When an adult reads a book like that to young children we expose them to an abundant vocabulary. The children will experience beautiful, well written sentences and they will have no problem following the plot. Charlotte Mason's students were able to read Dickens' books independently by the fifth and sixth grade because they had been exposed to high level literature early.

It is important to obtain the unabridged versions of the classics. In fact, that is one definition of a "whole" book. When the author wrote the whole book he did not anticipate that someone else would edit his work into a junior classic. Nor did he foresee a mere chapter of his work appearing in an English textbook without its surrounding content.

Another definition of a whole book is an entire book on one topic. I have a whole book on hummingbirds. I also have a whole book on chipmunks. In both cases I have a book that the author has put his heart into. The writing is excellent and the material is thoroughly covered, enabling me and my children to retain the information presented. Contrast that with a short mention of hummingbirds or chipmunks somewhere in a child's science textbook. One obvious difference is there simply is not room in a textbook to cover one animal in-depth. The writing is usually not "clothed in literary language" as Charlotte stated. The passion is lacking as well. When an author tackles a subject and is able to write an entire book on it, it is typically a topic which he is passionate about.

"Living books" is another common Charlotte Mason term. The easiest way to remember what makes a book a "living book" is to think of the word "alive." Basically, when people are alive they marry, have children, live out their lives and even die. One of my favorite examples of a living book is *Conversations with Pioneer Women*, by Fred Lockley. The author interviewed women in the Portland, Oregon area who had crossed the Oregon trail. Throughout the book as the women retell their experiences, tragedies occur—one of them is the disease cholera. At the close of the book you and your children will be well acquainted with that illness and will be able to tell others the rest of your life why it was indeed a tragic part of crossing the country. Again, contrast that with a paragraph dedicated to cholera in a history textbook. I doubt if a child would have the faintest idea of what the disease entailed even if you had taken the extra step of assigning it as a spelling word. When a connection is made by the child, especially an emotional connection, he can't help but remember the facts better. If retention is your goal then living books are your answer because they provide emotional connections.

Most interesting books bring about retention while boring books do not. That's why we avoid them whenever possible. The skill of assessing one from another is a valuable one you'll want to practice. Remember this method does not revolve around a certain book list and it does not revolve around only using books from the late 19th and early 20th centuries. Just because you blow the dust off a book in an antique store does not make it an interesting book. Charlotte's recommendations are older books because she lived a long time ago. But she wouldn't have been writing about boring, useless literature in her day if there wasn't any around.

Antique stores do have a lot of books and you could find all of your curriculum at one if you were choosy. Recently, I found two early 1900's spelling books complete with dictation exercises and I plan to use them. All of the school subjects are available in the antique stores. You'll find books on history, grammar, math, physics, botany, natural history, biographies, literally everything. However there is one drawback of using antique store books. They lack the quality of illustrations, photography and the updated knowledge available today.

Even when the illustrations in an older book are good, they are limited by the technology of the time. I have found combining an antique book with a modern book on the same topic to be extremely useful. For example if you're able to locate any English history books that Charlotte Mason recommended (or any interesting book), you'll encounter terminology that is new to children of the United States. When the book repeatedly refers to unfamiliar architecture like castles and moats, children will benefit from seeing pictures of these things. The solution is to find a current book with fabulous photography of castles and moats to augment the antique book.

Another example from my home school would be the Charlotte Mason recommended book, *Life and her Children*. Excellent book, inadequate illustrations. We supplemented this with a large beautiful book on sea life. If you were to add some quality videos or public television programming on underwater life and then spend some time observing a real sponge or visit an aquarium the book could really come to life.

This also works with classic literature such as *The Secret Garden*. Our family is currently reading that book which has frequent references to India. As an adult I'm well acquainted with the country, people and culture. I found my young children are not at all knowledgeable about India so we've been reading from Bobbie Kaufman's book, *India: The People*. This comes from a readily available, large set of books that cover many of the countries. They all have great photography and they are published by Crabtree Publishing Company.

You may have doubts about using whole books in the place of textbooks. This type of learning does not require previous practice, in fact, Charlotte wrote that everybody is capable of this approach. There was a common misconception of her day. Considerably large numbers of English people thought that a literary education was only comprehensible to the upper class. Charlotte disagreed and asserted that it is not dependent on social class or economic status.

Charlotte knew it was untrue because she worked with children and her observations led her to write, "because children who have little vocabulary to begin with, no trace of literary background, show themselves able to hear or read a work of literary value and after a single reading to narrate pages with spirit and accuracy . . . it signifies that a literary education is open to all, not after tedious and laborious preparation, but immediately. The people wait only for the right books to be put into their hands and the right method to be employed." (Vol. 6, p. 268)

A significant part of the "right method" is narration. It is pivotal to a Charlotte Mason education because it takes the place of questioning and easily verifies the knowledge of the student. Winston Churchill would have been thrilled to attend one of Mason's schools. Of his education he said, "I should have liked to be asked to say what I knew. They always tried to ask what I did not know. When I would have willingly displayed my knowledge, they sought to expose my ignorance. This sort of treatment had only one result: I did not do well in examinations." When it comes to examination time in Charlotte Mason's method we allow the child to expand on what they *do* know. Ordinary testing concentrates on what the student does not know, forgot, can't spell correctly or generally misconstrued. It can't help but be a negative experience when your "test" is graded and your abilities are determined by your mistakes.

Narration is not a Charlotte Mason invention. Evidently, Dr. Johnson had suggested the use of it one hundred years previously. (*Netta*, p. 38) Charlotte certainly capitalized upon the concept and helped us all immensely by showing us its usefulness in education.

Charlotte wrote that narration is "how we all learn, we tell again, to ourselves if need be, the matter we wish to retain, the sermon, the lecture, the conversation. The method is as old as the mind of man, the distressful fact is that it has been made so little use of in general education." (Vol. 6, p. 160)

Narration is very helpful to anyone who needs to improve their listening skills or reading comprehension skills. Both skills can be practiced, one by reading aloud and the other by having the student read independently.

Narration can be used orally or in the written form. More important than the format is to use this technique on a broad basis. Narration can be asked of a child who has been given a list of chores to complete. Ask him to repeat what you said to him—then he can't plead ignorance later.

A narration could be asked for after a day, week, month or year spent on a topic. Simply ask the student to tell you everything he knows about that topic. It's very effective for math, science and field trips. There is literally no end to the ways it can be applied. Remember, it is the narrator's mind that is primarily acting on the material. The listener's mind may also be acting on the material, if the same event was experienced however, it's crucial that the listener keep his thoughts to himself. That is the only way to grant acceptance of the other person's narration. Listen without comment but *do try to look like you are listening*. It's easy for narrations to be become mundane and it's tempting to open mail while you're supposedly listening. Keep that "I'm listening" face going at all costs.

Remember that different people have different thoughts. If two people narrated this book when they finished reading, we would expect two different narrations. Because no one would want to hear the book narrated in its entirety the narrator has to make split second decisions in an attempt to bring out the most pertinent facts and that in itself is the amazing thing about narrations.

If your student struggles with narration usually one of two things is happening. He does not know the material so he can't narrate it or he is not cooperating. The second is a disciplinary problem and needs to be handled as one.

Talkative people over-narrate and the reverse is true. You may find it helpful to model a narration for your child. One day without warning tell them you're in the mood to do the narrating today. Make it look easy, this is no time to show off. This is the best cure for over- and under-achievers. Another solution is to try a variety of books until the child finds one he can get excited about. This will help the narrations improve.

Don't forget narration is an easy and normal function that we've all used. We have all used this process when we've told someone about a meeting we have attended, a documentary we've seen or a book we have read. That is why it is also called retelling.

The act of repeating information or events has a powerful effect on memory, much like when we repeat a number over and over to ourselves when we are unable to write it down. Again, it's different from summarizing information because we allow the person narrating to choose the emphasis, even the omissions.

Often it isn't until the narration happens that the emotional connection is made with the material. A woman from Utah recently confirmed this. She had attended a workshop during which I had an emotional passage read to the audience in order for them to try a written narration of their own. I used a true "tear-jerker" passage which took ten minutes to read making it easy for the participants to write about. It also proves my point that emotional stories help people to remember the facts better. According to this particular lady it wasn't until that evening when she narrated the story to her husband that she really broke down and felt emotion about it.

Narration helps you to know exactly what your child retained about any given topic by focusing on what the child does know which can greatly increase any teacher's time. The test, pop quiz, chapter checkup and the book report are all replaced by something more effective.

Special education teachers are currently utilizing narration. Research has shown that reading small portions to developmentally delayed, downs syndrome, autistic children, etc. and then asking them to repeat what they heard has actually increased I. Q. points. Narration is also helping with auditory processing, a skill often lacking in special needs people. Not only that, but comprehension itself is a struggle with special needs people and this offers a better opportunity to succeed than traditional comprehension questions because it leads to "original thought" another skill commonly missing in that population. For a more information on the general use of narration see my first book, *A Charlotte Mason Education*.

The Charlotte Mason method encompasses many other topics such as being outside to a great extent, coupled with keeping a nature diary. She used extremely effective techniques in the language arts. All of these were covered in my first book. Her students also kept a book of the centuries and used short lessons, both of which are covered in greater detail in this book.

Recognizing and capitalizing on how habitual people tend to be is another of Mason's teachings. This teaching helps to pinpoint problem areas and offers tangible solutions to them. Charlotte asked her readers to reflect on how difficult life would be if we had to think through each routine action instead of relying on habit. In her words, "how the labour of life would be increased if every act of the bath, toilet, table, every lifting of the fork and use of spoon were a matter of consideration and required an effort of decision!" (Vol. 6, p. 101)

Recently, I had a chance to find out how true that is. We moved into a house that has a sink with reversed hot and cold water faucets. I thought I would grow accustomed to the reversal rather quickly—I was wrong. I would have been able to replace one habit with another if there had only been one sink in the house, however, it's not the only one and I admit I find myself in constant confusion when I'm in front of this particular sink. I have to "think" instead of relying on habit.

At our old house I had another chance to witness the power of habit when we moved the dining room clock and replaced it with a picture. Because the clock had hung there for nine years everyone found themselves disoriented by the change. I don't know how many times I stood in front of the picture mystified.

People operate cars through the power of habit as well. What would it be like to have to think about the turn signal, foot brake, steering wheel and two mirrors every time we made a turn? What does this have to do with education? Everything. Much of what we do, and how we do it, is controlled by habit. The key is to identify one bad habit at a time in yourself or your child and then purposefully replace it with a good habit. This is very effective and works in every area, including moral areas. I wrote about this in *A Charlotte Mason Education*, but when it came to moral and immoral decisions I wasn't as sure as I am now that this area is controlled by habit. I became convinced when I paid for my groceries with a hundred dollar bill. The clerk made change, wrapped it up inside the receipt and inadvertently included my hundred dollars. No one saw this, in fact, I almost didn't look at the wad myself. At the last moment I did look in my hand and saw what had happened. My reaction came so fast even I was surprised. One of my habits is honesty and it was out of habit that I returned the money. Later, I thought about Charlotte's teaching and I realized she was right again.

Charlotte Mason strongly believed that children are capable of making mental connections on their own. Her method is not typically regarded as a unit study approach however, it's easily combined with unit studies. Simply stated, a unit study is conducted by choosing a topic and covering it with a view to incorporate many school subjects simultaneously. One difference between the two philosophies is in a typical unit study Mom ties things together through careful planning—she makes the connections. In Charlotte Mason's method we have total confidence that the child will make the connections unassisted.

I've found that life is connected. Without planning, one topic (e.g. inventions, discoveries, etc.) may surface two or three times a day from a variety of books you're reading from. I've found this is also true with poetry—it's uncanny how random selections will augment teachings from other subjects covered earlier in the day. Currently in our home we are reading *The Secret Garden*, and by sheer coincidence we have planted our first garden. Recently, I bought *The Garden Game* and we are playing it daily. None of this was planned. I have grown accustomed to these kind of random choices coming together in a connected way.

If you enjoy planning and then proceeding on a well-thought out unit, then by all means, go ahead. I know families who wouldn't think of studying Idaho without making a big batch of potato salad at the conclusion of the unit.

You can't really offer an overview of the Charlotte Mason method without a mention of short lessons. Debates continue on whether this is an unschooling method or a structured one. (Unschooling represents learning through real life experiences rather than relying on a rigorous classroom replica.) Instead of taking one side or the other I would assert that this method is the best of both worlds. When a family uses short lessons in the morning they have lots of free time to follow a more unschooling type of lifestyle in the afternoon, by simply letting the child be on his own to pursue his own interests. Personally, I believe the afternoons, evenings and weekends provide ample time for hobbies and interests so I would never worry about conducting my home school with an interest led method. Charlotte's comment on the topic is, "I have throughout spoken of 'Relations,' and not of 'Interests,' because interests may be casual, unworthy, and passing. Everyone, even the most ignorant, has interests of a sort;" (Vol. 3, p, 241)

Do not let the ample free time become unproductive idle time. Staring into space is not a refreshing activity, in fact it's downright disturbing when you see someone doing it. (It makes you want to put a crossword puzzle book in their hands, at the very least.) Refreshment comes from variety and from changing your activity to something as different as possible from what you were doing. For example if you've been hand sewing on the couch and you need a rest, you don't set aside the project and then stare into space. You'd probably go outside and water the plants, take a walk or start a cooking project. If you've finished writing a long letter you don't refresh yourself by starting another long writing project. Provide the children with musical instruments, paint, paper, wood, gardening soil, sand, shovels, buckets and tons of books and they will occupy themselves in their free time.

In closing, what makes this Charlotte Mason method so popular anyway? I surveyed parents using this method from several of the English speaking countries and I have my own opinions. I believe the common thread would be that it provides a liberal (as in generous) education. Of course you have to teach the core subjects, but this method promotes the arts by including them and making time for them.

Most current home schooling parents were not home schooled and they were not presented with a humanities based education. They missed out and they know it. This is their chance to incorporate the finer things of life into their own education, plus enrich their children. Anybody can include classical literature, music and poetry but no other method provides a more fulfilling way to home school while using an effective way to retain information. No other method that I've heard of cares as much about the children and their involvement with the arts and nature. Meanwhile Mom is able to avoid burnout and use Charlotte Mason techniques any way she wants to, one hundred percent of her time or one percent. She is free to structure the school day or run things in a relaxed manner.

Extremes should be avoided, they do not work well. There are families who have taken the term "relaxed" a little too far. For some the distinction between unschooling and not schooling at all is completely blurred resulting in uneducated children who aren't taught basic math, geography, the calendar or even their own addresses. Others spend too much time chasing fads and seem to be consumed with learning *about* home schooling but do not seem to *apply* their knowledge in their homes. I believe it's beneficial to be well prepared but a person must remember that educating their children is a responsibility and it's hard work. The problem with fads is often they are unrealistic and unpractical.

The good news is Charlotte Mason won't be in your home and she won't know what you *do* or *don't* use from her method. So, the most important thing I can teach you in this book is to adapt her philosophy until it's your own. Take what you like and leave the rest alone. Never make a decision to please others—this isn't a popularity contest. You've probably already found this method provides many techniques that will alleviate the long hum-drum days spent teaching children. Find those that work for you and adapt them in any way that makes you comfortable.

I advocate two things. Combine educational methods to your liking and practice consistency. I believe this to be a successful formula and I still strongly believe we can succeed at home education and enjoy ourselves too.

Inspiration is better than condemnation. There are wonderful quotations from great people that help me when I feel like giving up. I respond well to what Charlotte wrote on page 135 of *Philosophy of Education*, "What the spring is to the year, school days are to our life . . . because that which we get in our youth we keep through our lives."

THREE

What Are The Liberal Arts?

A few years ago I discovered that the majority of home educating parents could not define a liberal education or the liberal arts. Perhaps the confusion lies with the word "liberal." For the most part, liberal, is thought of as the opposite of conservative. However, in this context we are referring to a broad, wide, generous education.

Anyone who teaches children should think about the purpose of education. Teachers and parents (and those who are both) need goals and priorities and need to know what we are trying to accomplish with the young people in our care. Robert Hutchins wrote about the fact that since the United States made the commitment to compulsory education the "object appears to be to keep the child off the labor market and to detain him . . . until we are ready to have him go off to work." (*The Great Conversation,* p. 24)

I have never met a home schooling parent who held to the above goal. Instead, I think most would agree with these sentiments from the

25

Parents National Education Union (PNEU). "No other part of the world's work is of such supreme difficulty, delicacy and importance, as that of parents in the right bringing up of their children. The first obligation of the present—that of passing forward a generation better than ourselves—rests with parents."

That's precisely what most of us want to do for our children. In one way or another, we want to provide a better life and a better education than we experienced. This seems to be part of the sacrifice of parenting. In the words of Robert Browning,

> "My poet holds the future fast,
> Accepts the coming ages' duty,
> Their present for this past."

Hutchins also did not think the purpose of education was mere detainment, in fact, the core message of his book was his concern regarding the disappearance of liberal education. Later he wrote, "Imagine the younger generation studying great books and learning the liberal arts. Imagine an adult population continuing to turn to the same sources of strength, inspiration and communication. We could talk to one another then. We should be even better specialists than we are today because we could understand the history of our specialty and its relation to all the others." (ibid. p. 31)

Now that is a valid educational goal! I've met math and science majors who believe their education was the direct opposite of a liberal arts education. Perhaps the process was the opposite, it depends on whether the schools they attended "specialized" too early. The earlier vocational training enters a young person's education the less liberally educated he will be. A broad base is needed before the specialty is targeted, that's how to understand where one's profession fits in relation with every other field. Graduates also need to be aware that math and science are included in the liberal arts so they cannot be considered opposites.

My goal is to give an accurate, working definition of the liberal arts so that you may be able to articulate and defend your educational philosophy. As I've already pointed out, many people do not have any kind of definition, and unfortunately the very few who do tend to have the wrong one.

Let's briefly review the history of education starting with the beginning. Writing began about 3000 B.C. After this breakthrough schools were developed, and *only* the exceptional boys were allowed to attend. Girls occasionally were taught how to read and write at home.

Early on the Hebrew people required *all* boys to attend school regardless of economic status. The girls were taught at home by their mothers.

The Greeks made the biggest advances in education, and our system is still based upon the one they developed. By 400 B.C. the Athenian education consisted of philosophy (which included math, science and logic) and rhetoric. At this point, though, the girls were still at home.

It was the Romans who first included girls up to the age of ten, however, the boys continued their school attendance into secondary school and eventually reached the stage of rhetoric.

Christianity is credited with causing a worldwide spread of education. During the middle ages the liberal arts were divided into two groups, the trivium and the quadrivium, also known as the *seven liberal arts.*

The trivium contained grammar, logic and rhetoric. Many medieval institutions taught only the trivium, and it was taught in Latin. These institutions mainly studied grammar and literature. After students worked in the trivium for three to four years, and if they passed the examination, then they would become a bachelor of arts. Another two or three years of study, and they would receive a teaching degree called a master. Sounds rather familiar doesn't it?

The quadrivium was arithmetic, astronomy, geometry and music. Some sources also list ancient languages, literature, divinity and philosophy (which included physics, ethics and religion). Other sciences were added as they were discovered.

Almost *all* the early universities studied the liberal arts and theology. During the Renaissance era only the wealthy European boys attended secondary school, and they were taught the liberal arts as well. Books were not readily available until the invention of the printing press in 1440. That did change everything but we need to remember that due to the scarcity of books, the poor only attended primary school while the affluent continued their education into the secondary level.

The reason we need to understand the exact order of events is because we need to understand the origin of a liberal arts education. To understand it, is to know that it was used to develop the upper-class and to cater to their intellect. Contrast this with what are called the practical (useful) arts that were designed for the lower class. In my research, the word "elitism" appeared as one explanation of why we now steer away from the term liberal arts.

Dennis Quinn also asserted that the liberal arts preceded the practical arts in his work, *The Integration of Knowledge, Discourses on Education.* He wrote, "Although the human condition consists mainly of work, and work is of the greatest importance to a satisfying and useful life, human existence is not *for* work (as it is in Marxist philosophy)."

With a liberal education we're talking about knowledge for knowledge's sake versus an education geared solely for vocational training. Roxanne Sitler wrote, "This pagan view looks at man as a resource, having no independent value apart from his ability to contribute to the state." (*Corporate America and Their Interest in Restructuring American Education*, p. 8)

Robert Hutchins says that the liberal arts are "an end in itself, for no other purpose than it would help them to be men, to lead human lives, and better lives than they would otherwise be able to lead." He also says, "The aim of liberal education is human excellence."

Hutchins does not agree that we should view education with an aim to an occupation, especially not an occupation determined during childhood. He stresses that it is the very rare person, with a very special talent, who will actually stay with an occupation chosen during childhood. He was very concerned with gearing the classroom around the child's interests; he sites the occupation of cowboy (apparently the leading choice of his day) as his example of how ridiculous it would be to aim all the intellectual material to that interest, or even to apprentice the pupils in that occupation. "The study of occupations as central in education assigns them a place to which they are not entitled."

Hutchins goes on, "The result of liberal education [is that the student learns] to read, write, speak, listen, understand and think. He learns to reckon, measure and manipulate matter, quantity, and motion in order to predict, produce, and exchange." My question is, what occupation could not benefit from people with these abilities?

Hutchins thinks that "we are all liberal artists, whether we know it or not. We all practice the liberal arts, well or badly, all the time every day." In other words, he is informing us that the liberal arts are unavoidable. Because of this he thinks the only question is whether we choose to remain ignorant and undeveloped or to "reach to the highest point" that we are capable of attaining. To summarize his thoughts, "The liberally educated man has a mind that can operate well in all fields."

Our last quote from Hutchin's work is amazingly similar to Charlotte Mason's ideals. He wrote, "The substance of liberal education appears to consist in the recognition of basic problems, in knowledge of distinctions and interrelations in subject matter, and in the comprehension of ideas."

The astute Charlotte Mason reader will no doubt recognize some similarities. As Charlotte states in *A Philosophy of Education*, "We, believing that the normal child has powers of mind which fit him to deal with all knowledge proper to him, give him a full and generous curriculum, taking care only that all knowledge offered to him is vital, that is, that facts are not presented without their informing ideas. Out of this conception comes our principle that:— 'Education is the Science of Relations'; that is, a child has natural relations with a vast number of things and thoughts: so we train him upon physical exercise, nature lore, handicrafts, science and art, and upon many living books." (Vol. 6, p. 154) Charlotte Mason also points out that none of this is dependent on social/economic class or cleverness.

Mason also reasoned that if the educational goal was merely to produce a literate citizen then what "we offer is too utilitarian,—an indirect training for the professions or for a craftsman's calling with efforts in the latter case to make a boy's education bear directly on his future work." (Vol. 6, p. 156)

Vocational training is being applied to public school classrooms as never before. With the twenty–first century comes a new direction in education known by several different names. I have not joined the others who predict the outcome of these changes because I don't believe any of us really knows the end results.

I do know this, our country already went through an educational upheaval during the industrial revolution when it decided school should be the training ground for factory workers. The current trend had targeted the year 2000 and originally the intention was to better supply corporate America with an improved work force. This may explain the focus on assessing elementary school students with the view to determine a vocation. Another assessment may take place during junior high followed by actual vocational training in the place of what we previously thought of as the high school years. It has been said that our current educationalists know they will "lose" a generation during the transition. An acquaintance of mine who is concerned about these changes often asks, "Whose children are they anyway?"

Charlotte goes right to the heart of the controversy when she wrote that the child "has a natural desire to know the history of his race and of his nation, what men thought in the past and are thinking now; the best thoughts of the best minds taking form as literature, and at its highest as poetry . . . It is a *wide* programme founded on the educational rights of man; wide, but we may not say it is impossible nor may we pick and choose and educate him in this direction but not in that. We may not even make [a] choice between science and the 'humanities.' Our part it seems to me is to give a child a vital hold upon as many as possible of those wide relationships proper to him. Shelley offers us the key to education when he speaks of 'understanding that grows bright gazing on many truths.'" (Vol. 6, p. 157)

Charlotte said at an Ambleside conference in England, "Let us be up and doing. Let us do *battle* with the schools for a liberal education." Why would an aging, sickly woman stand before an audience and put forth such a strong statement? Most likely because she thought, "Our education in all classes of society has become mechanical with only little interludes of interest . . . the people, are educated up to a certain point, but are not as they would say themselves 'the better of it!' Education has failed to bring to any class of society, as a class, new interests, keen mental enjoyment, aesthetic pleasure, elevation of character, principles of conduct." (*In Memoriam of Charlotte M. Mason*, p. 9) In the same book it was said of her that "it was 'for the children' that she lived and worked and thus through her, generations of children have learnt the joy of a liberal education."

"Mechanical" is exactly what education becomes when job training interferes and takes a primary position. Vocational training is valuable and supremely necessary for most young people but only *after* a wide education has been presented. Charlotte wrote, "But the people themselves begin to understand and to clamour for an education which shall qualify their children for life rather than for earning a living. As a matter of fact, it is the man who has read and thought on many subjects who is, with the necessary training, the most capable whether in handling tools, drawing plans, or keeping books. The more of a person we succeed in making a child, the better will he both fulfill his own life and serve society." (Vol. 6, p. 3)

The end result of a Charlotte Mason education is the children "find knowledge so delightful that it becomes a pursuit and source of happiness for a lifetime."

FOUR

How Short Lessons are Applied in the Charlotte Mason Method

"*You* want the child to remember? Then secure his whole attention," Charlotte writes in *Home Education.* (Vol. 1, p. 156) Her definition of attention is summarized as "the whole mental force is applied to the subject in hand. This act, of bringing the whole mind to bear, may be trained into a habit at the will of the parent or teacher, who attracts and holds the child's attention by means of a sufficient motive." (ibid., p. 145) We as parents want to know how this is accomplished, how much of this is the child's responsibility, and how much of it is ours. We also want to know how to get our children to stop dawdling. One of the main complaints I hear from home schooling audiences is, "My child just sits there not completing his math assignment. He will sit in front of it for hours—right up to dinner time. He doesn't care." To which I always say—that's right he doesn't care, you care. *You* are the one who's distressed by it.

Paying Attention

The formation of good habits is one of the foundational teachings of Charlotte Mason. Although it is not our topic in this chapter, it does apply to our use of time in the school day. Charlotte teaches us that adults should not waste time and neither should children. She would have us teach them that it is their duty to use their time well. She inspires and convicts us when she writes, "It is a bad thing to think that time is our own to do what we like with. We are all employed; we all have duties, and a certain share of our time must be given to those duties." She goes on to say that drifting, rather than using our time effectively, causes failure "in examinations, in their professions, in the duty of providing for a family, in the duty of serving their town or their country, not because they are without brains, nor because they are vicious, but because they do not see that *to use time* is a duty. They dawdle through the working day, hoping that some one will *make* them do the thing they ought." (Mason's emphasis) Ultimately, it is the children's choice to do their work without dawdling. Good habits will help you achieve this. Teach your children that there is "satisfaction to do the day's work in the day, and be free to enjoy the day's leisure." (Vol. 4, pt. 1, p. 173)

The power of attention is a very useful resource for any person to develop. As a parent, you want your children to listen to and retain the information you communicate to them. Charlotte points out that educated professionals, such as lawyers, have to be able to listen (pay attention) and react. "Contrast this with the wandering eye and random replies of the uneducated;—and you see that to differentiate people according to their power of attention is to employ a legitimate test." (Vol. 1, p. 137) Can you imagine communicating with your lawyer only to find out he or she was not paying any attention? How about with friendships? We all have friends who are good listeners, and we all have friends who are poor listeners—which kind of friend do we prefer?

Do not depend upon the will of the child to accomplish the development of attention. Depend upon habit. If your children are still young then I strongly recommend you read Charlotte's entire first volume, *Home Education* as soon as possible. You will find when reading it that these habits can, and should, be taught to our babies. Parents can help their children to play with one toy for just a little while longer than they would have without any guidance. This helps to train children at a young age to really look at things.

Variety Brings Refreshment

When a child gets older, "never let the child dawdle over a copy-book [penmanship] or sum, sit dreaming with his book before him. When a child grows stupid over a lesson, it is time to put it away. Let him do another lesson as unlike the last as possible, and then go back with freshened wits to his unfinished task." When the child returns to the lesson, it is now the parent's job to help "pull him through; the lesson must be done, of course, but must be made bright and pleasant to the child." (ibid., p. 141)

In the Charlotte Mason method we always vary the lessons to keep them fresh—in other words, to avoid boredom. It is invigorating to go from math to poetry, from penmanship to history. Choose the school subjects so that they alternate between painstaking lessons (e.g., they already know the material but they need further practice) and subjects that take thought. With each day's schedule we should strive to vary the order somewhat to avoid any drudgery of a strict routine.

How Much Time is Allotted?

This method includes the posting of a schedule, which should indicate what to do and how long each lesson will last. Having our schedule posted on the wall has proven to be a successful addition to our home school week. It is true that we all function at our best when we know what is going to come next and what is expected of us. Charlotte writes, "Again, the lessons are short, seldom more than twenty minutes in length for children under eight." (ibid., p. 142)

The use of short lessons provides for each subject being fifteen to twenty minutes in length during elementary school. They increase to thirty minutes per subject in junior high and to forty-five minutes in high school. Remember, the Charlotte Mason students were in school six days a week, and they were covering fifteen to twenty-one subjects per week, even as early as seven and eight years of age. If you need additional time for any subject, you may want to add another short segment at some other time in your day or weekend. You can also try teaching some of the material that will be new to the child during other times and then using short lessons for practicing what they do know.

Sufficient Motivation Without Bribery

How should we try to motivate our students to finish their lessons promptly? One important thing that Charlotte Mason suggested was that we not just rely on one or two motivations even if they seem to work. Instead she taught that we should "incite the child to effort through his desire of approbation, of excelling, of advancing, his desire of knowledge, his love of his parents, his sense of duty, in such a way that no one set of motives be called unduly into play." (ibid., p. 141)

While keeping the above list in mind, we should note Charlotte's emphasis on the schedule described in the previous section. This motivates the child because he knows that there is not much time to complete his assignment. This helps to keep the child alert. This is particularly helpful when dealing with the child's least favorite subject. It's sort of the "eat-your-spinach" concept. If he doesn't like it, at least he knows once it is finished he won't be asked to do it again until tomorrow.

I've never seen this advice in any of Charlotte Mason's books, but I know from personal experience that some people, both young and old, are motivated by being able to cross tasks off a list, or drawing a line through the completed assignment of the planning book. Some parents like to use the motivational charts that are sold at teacher stores, which includes the use of stickers. Even if this has never appealed to you, there is a chance that one of your children might be highly motivated by the satisfaction of filling in a chart.

What we can know is that Charlotte did recommend the use of natural rewards. The example she gives in *Home Education* on page 143 is of a child being allowed twenty minutes to complete his math. If he gets it done quickly and correctly then the "natural consequence[s] of his good conduct" is that he has a few minutes of leisure time. Charlotte says that he can choose any activity including a quick trip outside or drawing. I, too, would give him the rest of the time to draw or do whatever he enjoys that does not distract the other children. At our house we keep enjoyable things right in the child's school box so that he can quietly occupy himself without breaking the attention of anyone else in the room.

Schools have relied upon the giving of letter grades or marks as Charlotte called them, for motivation. Charlotte Mason is against giving marks and most home schooling parents neither bother nor approve of them. In fact, Charlotte Mason would prefer that we teach our children if they come in first at something to not be vain about it, and if they happen to come in last at something to not have bitterness. We are to bring up our children to have so much "love and sympathy that joy in his brother's success takes the sting out of his own failure, and regret for his brother's failure leaves no room for self-glorification." Charlotte Mason counsels us that if we are going to use grades "as a stimulus to attention and effort, the good marks should be given for conduct rather than for cleverness—that is, they should be within everybody's reach: every child may get his mark for punctuality, order, attention, diligence, obedience, gentleness." I agree with Charlotte's alternative ideas for grades but even so, she ends this teaching by reminding her readers that *any* grades distract the children's attention away from their work. The assignments we give them should be interesting "enough to secure good behavior as well as attention." (ibid., p. 144)

When a child gets older he has to make himself pay attention. "He should be taught to feel a certain triumph in compelling himself to fix his thought." (ibid., p. 145) Later in *Home Education* she tells us to, "Let him enjoy a sense of triumph, and of your congratulation, whenever he fetches his thoughts back to his tiresome sum, whenever he makes his hands finish what they have begun." (ibid., p. 328)

Your job as the home schooling parent is to make sure that your "child never does a lesson into which he does not put his heart." (ibid., p. 146) This will build the habit of finishing that Charlotte writes about in *Ourselves*. One of my favorite quotes of hers is, "What is worth beginning is worth finishing, and what is worth doing is worth doing well." (Vol. 4, pt. II, p. 172) She knows it's tempting to start something new, but she insists that "It is worth while to make ourselves go on with the thing we are doing until it is finished." Adding, "Let us do each bit of work as perfectly as we know how, remembering that each thing we turn out is a bit of ourselves, and we must leave it whole and complete; for this is Integrity. The idle, the careless, and the volatile may be engaging enough as companions, but they do not turn out honest work, and are not building up for themselves integrity of character. This rests upon the foundations of diligence, attention, and perseverance. In the end, integrity makes for gaiety, because the person who is honest about his work has time to play, and is not secretly vexed by the remembrance of things left undone or ill done." (ibid., p. 172) Obviously, this applies both to the children and to the parents. In fact, I have gone back to this quote more than once for motivation to finish what I have started, namely, home schooling itself and helping people learn how to do the Charlotte Mason method. To me both were worth starting so they are worth finishing.

The Stubborn Dawdler

Even though Charlotte Mason suggested that the child start the day with math because his brain would be the most fresh, I find when I talk to struggling mothers that math is one of the most despised subjects. So, for the *very extreme cases* where a child has turned dawdling into an Olympic sport, I suggest saving math for the last subject of his school day. You may be able to offer something even more tantalizing at the end of his day rather than in the middle. If he likes to play basketball with the neighborhood boys when they come home from school, then planning his math time to coincide with their arrival could be the best motivation for him, provided, of course, he correctly completes his assignment within the given twenty, thirty or forty–five minutes. You could also set up a board game, the paint and brushes, or whatever he most enjoys next to where he is working, to be ready for him as soon as his lesson is over. This teaching is explained on page 147 of *Home Education.*

Even a particularly difficult child can be enticed to apply his mind as best as he can. Laura C. Faunce wrote, "We of the PNEU hold, and experience has proved to me over and over again, that all children are receptive of the right kind of knowledge rightly introduced, and *no matter how despairing* one may be of a child, one has always the joy of the sudden revelation, when the vital spark has been struck." (*In Memoriam of Charlotte M. Mason,* p. 167) Again, I want you to always keep in mind that the material itself is to be relied on eventually, and you do not want to enter into an elaborate system of bribery.

Obstinate refusal to cooperate with the home schooling parent, after sufficient motivation and interesting school work has been provided, is a discipline problem and needs to be handled as such. I would suggest your home school principal be consulted and the problem remedied in whatever manner with which you usually train your children when they have directly defied your authority. I use the demerit system at our house. It helps me to write down the offending behavior and post it where our principal (Dad) will see it when he gets home. Don't get me wrong here, I do not rely on my husband to do all the disciplining—I do my fair share in any given week. In addition to this, however, it seems to be effective for my children to know that their demerit is hanging on the wall and that I can always add further offenses. I balance this by bringing the children's accomplishments to their father's attention as well—when a good attitude was exhibited or something was mastered by one of the children that day.

Of strengthening the will of the child, Charlotte Mason wrote, "Every effort of obedience which does not give him a sense of *conquest* over his own inclinations, helps to enslave him." Instead, she tells us to "invite his co-operation, let him heartily intend and purpose to do the thing he is bidden, and then it is his own will that is compelling him, and not yours; he has begun the greatest effort, the highest accomplishment of human life—the making, the compelling of himself." (Vol. 1, p. 328) That, incidentally, is my all-time, favorite quote from Charlotte Mason's writings.

This idea of short lessons is often approached with skepticism by parents; I know, I was a doubter myself. I have often asked parents this question, "Do you have anything to lose by trying it? If you were to try short lessons and find they did not work for you, couldn't you just go back to long lessons?" I cannot even count the number of parents who tried this and now rave about short lessons.

As with narration, don't make using short lessons more complicated for yourself than it has to be. It can be very simple, and it allows you to get around to all those really good living books, art prints and music you've collected.

You'll find some of my former schedules in the appendix so that you can see how I implement short lessons. When I created my latter schedules my oldest child had finished home school, so it represents the three students I had that were between first and sixth grade. (I also had an active, demanding, pre-school age child at the time.) Ample time is allowed between subjects to ensure the necessary materials are located and ready to use. In the chapter on planning you'll find my thoughts on how to correlate scheduling with using short lessons and an explanation of how to adjust your schedule to cope with interruptions.

The latter schedules may look like we're in school all day but it provides a nice, leisurely pace. When I need to, I am able to move through the schedule a little more quickly, cut back on the between-subject breaks, skip the morning recess and complete the school day before lunch. By providing this glimpse into our home school, my hope is that you'll see how short lessons can be used, be motivated to try them, and see for yourself how valuable they are to a full and rich curriculum.

FIVE

Segment Planning

$\mathscr{T}$here are both structured and unstructured families using the Charlotte Mason method. This is a personal choice that each family is entitled to make for themselves. Some, rather than gravitating clearly to one or the other, sway between the two perhaps undecided on which framework is best for them. I read an amusing article entitled *Homeschooling Schizophrenia*[1] by Diane Flynn Keith. She writes that because she was originally inspired by John Holt she started as an unschooler and continues with, "Sometimes, though, a homeschool panic attack would disrupt this rapturous scene. Usually it was incited by the kid-next-door who came over and said he got an A+ on his long division test, or that he just finished writing a five-page report on the Industrial Revolution.

---

[1] The article *Homeschooling Schizophrenia* was quoted with permission from *The Link—A Homeschool Newspaper*, Vol. Two, Issue Four. This free publication may be obtained by calling (805) 492-1373. The author, Diane Flynn Keith, edits and publishes *Homefires—The Journal of Homeschooling*, and she may be contacted by calling (888) 4-HOME-ED or go to www.homefires. com.

Sometimes it occurred because a grandparent (after taking the kids to a movie) questioned why the children were having trouble reading the credits that were in cursive type on the movie screen. It had even happened when another homeschooling friend proudly shared that her 13-year-old daughter successfully passed the high school proficiency exam. During these episodes something deep inside me would well up and transform me into a ruler-swinging school marm ready to 'drill and kill' my kids all the way to college. I'd announce that, 'things are going to change around here.' I'd get on the phone and order catalog curriculum products. I'd create a schedule of subjects, neatly align the materials we'd need, and begin a rigid program of structured learning. My kids looked at me like I was nuts but cooperatively went along with my antics—for a while. Usually about three weeks into the packaged-curriculum-product-paces my kids revolted. They would object, whine, complain, and beg for a reprieve. When I was finally exhausted from the demand of lesson preparations and had been thoroughly worn down from the kids' pitiful whining and misery—my alter-ego emerged. You know, the 'let's take the day off and go to the beach' unschooler who squelched the tenured-teacher ego and encouraged the kids to play hooky." The author continued her article with a message of balance and that is what I believe all home schoolers are searching for—a happy medium.

I have heard from other home schooling mothers who, immediately after investing in an expensive, structured curriculum, found it to be a disaster. This is when I wish the parent had heard of the Charlotte Mason method before spending an inordinate amount of money. I am convinced that her method provides the perfect mixture of both concepts and you'll find both Charlotte Mason's books and her magazine, the *Parents' Review*, clearly showed a structured morning followed by an *unstructured* afternoon during which the children were free to be children and follow their own interests. The evenings were also free to be used constructively and not merely to be wasted in idle time; these too were accomplished with very little adult supervision.

Using short lessons and planning are how I have been able to get all the required subjects in and still have time for the humanities. If you attempt to plan your school year then I suggest you aim for the happy medium instead of going from one extreme to another.

Trimesters, Semesters or Quarters?

There are many ways the school year can be divided. Using trimesters is one option and they were used by Charlotte's schools. Basically, school is in session for three months and then everyone has one month off. Charlotte Mason's trimesters, or terms, lasted eleven weeks, at six days per week for a total of sixty–six days (198 days per year). The terms were named for the season it would be during the examination time; therefore, they were called the Christmas, Easter, and Summer terms. (The Summer term ended in the middle of July.)

Trimesters are not superior to quarters or semesters. Each system could be used in a relaxed way or a structured way depending on your preference. One realistic way to approach the school year is with bad weather, good weather plans, (if your weather changes). My weather changes from really rainy to not *as* rainy during the year. The heavy rain coincides with the shorter days so I concentrate on a stricter schedule during those months. During the "better" weather I still have school but it's conducted more in an unschooling approach. That gives me the balance between those two extremes.

Another option is to think in year round terms. First find out how many days you are required by law to have school in your state. In Washington state, where I live, the quantity is 180 days per year. When 180 is divided by 12 (months) you get the number 15. Meaning, I could teach 15 days per month and have 15 days off per month.

As the parent you could choose one or two terms a year where you are very involved with teaching the children and one term that they are learning completely independent from you. What a break that would be! The children are progressing, or at least not going backward, and you are relaxing or concentrating on your own interests.

One school year I patterned my schedule after the Charlotte's schools by using trimesters. Her advice had proven to be effective in every other area, so I duplicated her methods, followed a trimester system, and used many of the same books as described in Charlotte Mason's 1922 *Parents' Review* article, *The Work and Aims of the Parents' Union School*. I enjoyed devoting myself to home school for three months knowing I'd soon have a whole month off. My school year was September, October, November, with December off; January, February, March, with April off; and May, June, July, with August off. I also scheduled a week off in the middle of each trimester. Because variety is important I've only used trimesters for one year—I'm still experimenting with different schedules.

Planning for any length of time, a year, month or week, involves a lot of different concepts, and short lessons is one of them. You also need to know what your goals are for the year (which is your personal choice), break those down to segments (quarters, seasons, months, etc.), then go out and find the materials you'll need, or find materials within your own growing inventory at home.

Planning will help you to decide how and when to use all those really great books you've collected but may never get around to reading. I don't want to discourage you from collecting, but I do want you to be aware that it takes a long time to go through the kinds of books Charlotte recommended. While it is our "Charlotte Mason duty" to provide our children with the most interesting books, she would also want us to use them.

Creating a Timetable

Some example schedules can be found in the appendix and they are meant to be just that, examples. The good thing about using 15 minute increments on your timetable is how easy they are to double or triple to accommodate any junior or senior high children in the home. It means the older student will work longer on math, for instance, than the younger student so it's fairly easy to have him start fifteen minutes before everyone else starts and continue during the fifteen minutes the others are in math. That way he'll have the required thirty minutes. The older child can extend his dictation time (or any other subject) into lunch or after school, too.

When you plan your schedule remember to take everything into account, including any outside activities such as music lessons. (Try only accepting doctor appointments around your schedule just like you would do if your child went to public school or if you had a job you couldn't take time off from.) *You must do this first.* You may find there is far too much stuff you're signed up for. We've all known a "car schooler." Her children literally keep their books in the car and do the majority of their work on the go. I recommend you clear your weekly calendar completely if you intend to succeed at home education. Maybe, allow one or two activities per week, if you're able to stay disciplined (by that I mean, continue to teach the other days of the week).

I know some of you are thinking this is a bit harsh. After all you've enjoyed home school band, piano lessons, skating, drama, foreign language, art lessons and the occasional home school luau. These are good things, you're thinking, I can't possibly eliminate any of them. I know, I've been there. In fact I've been there for ten years now and clearing the schedule is always a hard thing to do. But this is also ten years experience telling you that my best home schooling years have been those spent at home with the curtains drawn and the phone unplugged. Home schooling parents do not feel good about themselves when they've knowingly neglected the education they have taken responsibility for. You may not agree with me, but it is my opinion that *too many outside activities* makes you feel like you're not doing enough home school. I've also seen this elicit a sense of failure in some parents. That, in turn, may cause you to seek more outside help, such as tutors, to compensate. That's what I'd call a viscous circle.

When creating a schedule remember to incorporate variety—it

brings refreshment to everyone involved. Variety is the reason the Charlotte Mason schools did not get hung up on one curriculum, they wanted the days to be fresh and the materials to be fresh.

You should stagger the subjects so that the children alternate between painstaking lessons, practice lessons and reading lessons. For instance, have them do something like math or handwriting, then you can read aloud to them. After they narrate they could work with their hands, followed by more reading and narrating. Then they could work on their geography or recitation and then another reading session.

Keep in mind there are two ways to schedule and still have plenty of variety. One way is to have the children work independently for a substantial length of time (like an hour) and then consolidate the time you read aloud to them into one longer session using many different books covering science, history, literature and poetry. If you find your children are bored by an hour long reading time and find it too difficult to sit still then try sprinkling the readings in throughout the school day.

There are other advantages to sprinkling the read alouds in among the independent work—not only are the children fresher during the entire school day as was the original idea, but the parent has "free time" off and on during the school day. You'll find you have a few minutes to catch up on the mail or some other chore, but try to occupy yourself with something that can be easily interrupted because the children are apt to have questions. If you haven't planned the next teaching lesson, you have fifteen to twenty minutes to get out the materials you'll need and start looking them over.

The alternating method works well for another reason. Sometimes we do not follow through on our good intentions. If we have the children doing all of their independent work at one time, that gives mom an hour to get involved with other priorities in the home. When it comes time to spend a solid hour reading from the history book, the Bible, the science book and do art study, something usually gives and, nine times out of ten, it's the humanities. It becomes too easy to justify quitting for the day because the child has covered the basics (independent work often includes math and handwriting) and then the decision is made to forgo the humanities for "just one more day."

If you have a preschool child or a special needs child alternating independent segments with parental involvement segments works well. It is much easier to have a little one occupy himself for fifteen to twenty minutes at a time, especially if he knows he'll have you to himself for a whole twenty minutes in a short while. Another useful practice that has helped us stay disciplined one year was wearing inexpensive, matching, T-shirts of the same color during school hours. It really helps everyone (preschoolers and special needs children especially) to know that it's school time, and it's not free time until the school shirts are removed.

Make sure to stagger the books you read from. When I first got a copy of *Jack's Insects* (a book C. Mason highly recommended, now out of print) I intended to read it cover to cover to my children. As interesting as that book may be it reads better when we take a short break from it. We keep the days fresh by having two or even three science books and history books we're reading from. You can read from one of them for a couple of weeks or a couple of days and then switch to one of the others. It turns out that Charlotte Mason used *Jack's Insects* the same way. They read from it not *through* it.

Using a Planning Book

If you really want smooth weeks for yourself or need to become more accountable then buy a teacher planning book and *use* it. Some of my best school years have been accomplished with careful planning. Because I have never cared for written instructions, such as you find in curriculums, I had avoided using teacher planning books because I assumed I wouldn't want to read and follow even my own instructions. I was wrong—the difference is that I have customized it for my family and made it easy to follow. Each day I looked forward to opening my planning book because everything had already been decided and was well thought out. It was worth the effort, and I came to rely on it.

You can either buy one for each child capable of using it independently or buy one for yourself to use as a master plan for all of your children. The disadvantage with individual planning books is that you have to write much of the same content in multiple books.

This is no time to forgo the variety factor—keep that utmost in your mind when you fill in your planning book. Let's take science as an example. If you looked at one of my former planning books you'd see that in any given week I'd read from Anna Comstock's chapter on birds in her *Handbook of Nature Study*, Edmund Selous' *Jack's Insects*, and *Greenhead* (a book on ducks). For variety we drilled our bird identification cards once a week in place of a reading. But remember, the only way to finish a book is to read it on a consistent basis. It may take a little longer to complete books this way, but it gives us the variety we're striving for. Those kinds of literary science books combined with nature walks and nature diaries gave us variety. As the year progressed I replaced those science books with *Life and Her Children, Chipmunks on the Doorstep,* and once or twice a week we used *Ring of Fire, Igneous Rocks,* by Myrna Martin which is a hands-on (rocks and hand microscope included) geology kit.

What Will a Planning Book Do For You?

A planning book will make short lessons work better for you and help keep you accountable to your own ideals. If you have gone to the trouble to write in "Read Black Beauty chapter 35" and there is a date beside it you are more likely to read it rather than skip the reading when your phone rings.

Plan recesses and other breaks into your book. Quite often I plan a three-day weekend every week. Sometimes during the school week when I'm working hard, it helps me to persevere knowing that I'll have Friday off. I also think it would be wise to plan an entire week off in the middle of your trimester or semester. Wouldn't it be nice to know on some of your roughest home schooling days that you had some relax-ation time coming? Another reason to schedule a week off into your plan is if something unforeseen happens and you have to take a week off from school, you can then spare that time without ruining your whole plan. The same thing applies to my scheduling Friday off—if I miss a school day, I have a potential make-up day already there. In fact I use those Fridays to get in anything that was shoved aside during the week.

Make sure you don't get too ambitious and over plan—this will only discourage you. It may help you to start small and plan one week as an experiment. If you find that you have overdone anything on your schedule, such as the amount of time you spend reading out loud, then acknowledge it, eliminate some of it, and add it in next time you plan. With practice you'll easily decide whether it's best for you to plan for a week, a month or larger time frames.

To Date or Not to Date

In the planning book itself you can either date the entries or not date them, and that makes all the difference in the world. I have to suggest that if you've been unschooling for any length of time and this is your attempt to turn over a new leaf, do yourself a favor and do not use dates.

Not dating your entries makes it possible for you to skip a subject or an entire day. It also helps during times of family illness or life's inter-ruptions so that your planning book will not be all messed up. Using a planning book that isn't dated provides another way to cope—instead of skipping an entire day, you can look at your planning book and condense the assignments and the planned readings to a shorter time so that you still accomplish something. Then you can compensate the following day.

Whether you date your planning book or not, you can look at each book you plan to use for the next school segment and determine how many pages you'll be able to read in ten to twenty minutes, then write page numbers or chapter numbers into your planning book. After you've read from any given book, you will know whether a full chapter or a partial chapter constitutes the right amount of time. This is optional, but I find it very helpful for estimating when we will complete a book or a certain segment of a book. Or you can simply make an entry that states what books you are reading rather than exactly what page numbers or use a combination of each approach. *Only you know if you need more flexibility or more accountability.* If, in the past, you've tended toward skipping more school than you had planned, then remember that not dating your entries will make it easier to slip into bad habits. Dated entries help me to stick to my plan when I'd rather goof off. However, if at anytime you feel you are in danger of burning out, then by all means adjust your planning book rather than discarding the whole concept. Make it work to your advantage; you do not have to be a slave to it. (And always use a pencil!)

Becoming Accountable

For those of us who may need to apply ourselves more to this business of home schooling, then invite someone to become your accountability partner. Tell her your goals and have her ask you every Friday if you accomplished your goals that week. As she gets to know you, she will be able to tell you when you're beating yourself up for no reason or be honest and say you need to regroup and apply yourself more. In *A Charlotte Mason Education* I mentioned getting someone to commit to praying for you every single day; this could be the same person. Do you think someone wants to spend valuable time praying for you, while you never seem to get yourself disciplined?

Whether or not having an accountability partner is feasible, planning your time and following through brings a sense of satisfaction that you didn't shirk your responsibilities. Your children progressed a little and had a full day, full week and full year—in other words, a full education, including the humanities.

If at this point you're thinking, "Hey, I never read any of this in Charlotte Mason's books," or "I thought this was a unschooling method," or

"This looks like too much work!"

You would be right that the six-volume set does not have any extensive passages on how a trimester would be planned, that information is found in other Charlotte Mason materials such as her magazine and other PNEU publications.

As far as unschooling goes, Mason's method probably should not be considered one of the various forms of unschooling. It is a *far more relaxed method* than relying on textbooks, classical education or many other methods common to home schooling. Because the degree to which a family chooses to unschool is a personal decision my position is that you should take what you like from C. Mason's method and leave the rest out of your home school. Neither Charlotte nor I are going to be at your house policing your decisions.

On point number three let's remember that this method has not become popular because of its effortlessness. It's popular because both the parent and the child are exposed to more and learn more than with ordinary methods. Using Charlotte's philosophies including the way the mind processes, and is stimulated by the arts and other interesting information results in retention of knowledge and eliminates boredom. Meanwhile, Mom knows that she's done her best and that in itself is her reward.

I have some very good news for you at the close of this teaching. You will find after practicing short lessons and scheduling that the school day will start to fall into place. What I mean is the use of time scheduled segments will become natural and eventually you won't need to use the kitchen timer or the even the schedule itself. It's a satisfying feeling to watch your students working out of habit and when that time comes in your household you'll be glad you made the effort.

Finally, don't forget the balance! In the past I've had to correct myself and the tendency to relax too much through better planning. The reverse is also true. It feels really good to "fly by the seat of my pants" some of the time and give spontaneity a chance.

SIX

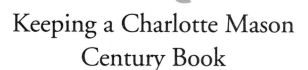

Keeping a Charlotte Mason Century Book

*M*ost home schooling families find history to be so interesting and enjoyable that it tends to be a very popular subject. However, even when we like this subject, we do have a few concerns. We wonder, "Am I teaching enough, covering it correctly, graduating children with 'gaps,' and how will they retain all that they have learned?"

Then there are those who view the subject of history itself to be among the most boring. Most likely, their memories are not that clear on what the material was they were supposed to be covering and the little bit they can recall might be those ugly lists of inventors' names, including the name of the invention and of course, the date it was invented. Everybody loves to memorize a list like that by Friday morning—don't they? How about all the wars and their dates? Memorizing lists is boring and it always will be. The problem is how to get kids to know their dates without the tears and boredom. The book of centuries provides a fun way for children to see from the beginning to the end and provides real context for the events they are studying.

The basis for my research on the book of centuries, or century book as referred to here, was found in an article written by Miss G. M. Bernau entitled *The Book of Centuries and How to Keep One.*[2] I have read this article many times over the last few years, and it serves as a very nice outline for learning how to keep a century book whether you choose to follow the PNEU guidelines precisely, as noted in the *Parents' Review* article, or adapt the concept to meet your own needs.

Bernau began her article with some well-chosen and highly inspirational quotes from Charlotte Mason regarding her thoughts on history. Without a doubt the most thought provoking of these were, "offer such a liberal and generous diet of History to every child in the country as shall give weight to his decisions, consideration to his actions and stability to his conduct; that stability, the lack of which has plunged us into many a stormy sea of unrest." (Vol. 6, p. 179) and "it is necessary to know something of what has gone before in order to think justly of what is occurring to-day." (ibid., p. 169)

The thoughts of Charlotte Mason bring to mind the quote, "Those who do not remember the past are condemned to repeat it." (George Santayana, *The Life of Reason.*) Not only is she correct, but she may have hit upon the problem existing within the United States public school system regarding history. It is possible that you received a well-rounded history education growing up, but I did not. Instead of teaching us "what has gone before," the emphasis was "social studies." The result, in my opinion, is that at least one generation slipped through with a high school diploma but without basic history. Thank goodness for home schooling—it has come to my rescue, and I credit it with the only history I've ever learned. If it were up to me I would not choose to live

---

[2] Originally printed in Charlotte Mason's *Parents' Review* magazine and reprinted in Karen Andreola's Fall 1992 issue of her *Parents' Review* publication.

among an entire generation that was doomed to repeat a history they had no knowledge of. A prime example would be gang participation. There is nothing new about it, and there is ample historical proof, (e.g., in *Plutarch's Lives*) that the world has had to contend with marauding groups of young violent people for a very long time.

Brief Review of Charlotte Mason's Approach to History

At this point we need to review a few basic Charlotte Mason techniques for teaching history. It is important to know that keeping a century book will be more successful if you are exposing the children to a wide variety of written material such as biographies, diaries, literature, plays, novels, essays and poems.

For example, you'll find that children retain a lot more about an inventor and his inventions when you read a biography of his life rather than memorizing a list of dry facts. That is what a living book accomplishes, retention. It's a foolproof approach because people remember things better when they make an emotional connection. Charlotte Mason always taught this and I already believed her when I saw a television program on the educational channel. As I remember it, some researchers took a large group of people through a slide show with someone acting as a narrator to the events they were watching. It was explained that they were watching an employee of a large firm leaving his place of work. As he exited the building he saw a huge accident scene right outside of the building. People were sprawled all over the ground and medical help had arrived. Each person viewed the slides alone but half of the group was told that the whole thing was a reenactment so that first aid skills could be practiced and the other half was told it was absolutely real. Several weeks later when the people returned to conclude their part of the research they were asked about the slide show. None of the people who were told it was merely a reenactment even remembered there was a such a presentation and the people who were told the opposite remembered with uncanny detail everything the narrator had said. An emotional connection had been made.

For the same reason well-written historical novels may be carefully considered and included from time to time in your history course. Be watchful for "doctored" accounts where heathens have become mighty men of God and for the reverse in which all Christianity is unnecessarily removed because of someone's agenda.

There are three things to keep in mind when selecting books. First, it is essential that the book be interesting rather than boring, living rather than dry. Second, the more first-hand accounts you can find the more accurate your study will be. Third, do not be afraid to challenge your children's minds by selecting above-grade-level books. Charlotte wrote that "Education implies a continuous going forth of the mind." (Vol. 6, p. 66)

Keep in mind the Charlotte Mason schools and home schools did not rely solely on books for their history lessons. They also used architecture, paintings of the period and encouraged visits to historical museums. Not every person reading this will have access to a museum, and I do not want you to be discouraged if you don't live near one. Perhaps, as finances allow, you could plan a family trip to where there are some good museums and national monuments, which were also recommended by Mason. If that is likely to be an infrequent event, she recommended looking at pictures of monuments if seeing them in person was not possible.

When using Charlotte Mason's strategy for teaching history we need to remember three other concepts she stressed. First, study other countries as early as possible to avoid an "arrogant habit of mind." Second, when studying a period, country or person try to compare what other people in other countries were doing at that same time. Finally, Charlotte Mason schools always studied history in chronological order.

My personal view on chronology is to apply it as I am studying a person, war or country. It is logical to study the events in the order that they really happened. I believe that we as parents are able to choose what we will cover and in whatever sequence we think best. In other words, I do not think it is necessary to study early civilizations with our young children working chronologically toward modern-day history in high school.

Covering ancient history at the younger grade levels presents at least two difficulties that I can see. The materials available in the United States for teaching our own history tend to be available to meet any age level. There is an abundance of materials about the pilgrims, the revolutionary war, the Oregon Trail, etc. that are suitable for younger students. I am well aware that we Charlotte Mason families attempt to bring adult-level reading material to the young student but there is a place and a time for them to read books written for children. I think reading historical accounts (or fiction) is an excellent use of time for the young reader, in addition to reading other types of books. In contrast, the written materials dealing with ancient times tend to be among the most difficult reading material available.

The second difficulty is the content of that material. As I said earlier it is the home schooling parent's prerogative to select the order in which they will cover history. That goes for content as well. As a Christian mother I am purposely choosing to leave the ancient history with all of its mythology until after my children are much older and therefore have been exposed to much more Biblical history. My conviction is that they will be able to make better sense of false gods and idol worship having had plenty of Old Testament teaching first. Again, this is my personal opinion, and I do not ask nor expect people to adopt my views.

For more information on how to use the Charlotte Mason approach for teaching history, please read *Home Education,* Vol. 1, pp. 279–295; *A Philosophy of Education*, Vol. 6, pgs. 169–180; or the condensed account in *A Charlotte Mason Education*, pgs. 63–68.

The Origin of Century Books

It is important to know that the earliest form of the century book was known as a Museum Note Book. It served as a combination sketchbook/notebook with each page representing a century. In 1915 Charlotte's home schools had transformed these into a book of centuries.

When you consider that drawing sketches of museum objects was one of the main objectives, it can easily remind you of the nature notebooks that Charlotte Mason children also kept. It appears that everything you can think of was sketched in these books. Some examples given were bowls, cups, ships, weapons, costumes, jewelry, musical instruments, clothing and historical events.

They also permitted photographs to be pasted in, but warned that if it was overdone the book would become bulky. I'm not concerned with bulkiness in regard to my children's books, but I do not want them to turn into scrap albums either. Newspaper cuttings were also allowed because current events were included. Bernau wrote that the "century book is a live thing of present, past and future tense. Each book is an individual work of intelligence and, very often, of art." However, just as with the nature notebooks, do not let a lack of artistic talent keep you from trying one. Bernau assured us that "There is no need to be an artist in order to have an interesting book—though neatness and accuracy are essential."

Making it a Habit

Because Bernau wrote the "book of centuries should bear witness to a 'liberal and generous diet of history'" and "also bear witness to some special study in museums each term," starting one for your child can motivate you to follow through on some good intentions. If you have access to museums then perhaps your visits can become more frequent. Bernau suggested that the children would view the museum objects more as "old friends" because they had previously sketched them. I have often asked people to imagine the average boy walking through a museum bored by a vast array of artifacts. He's is thinking to himself, "Yeah, yeah, another broken bowl. Big deal!" Picture that same boy recognizing the broken bowl and excitedly looking back in his book for the sketch he made a few years ago. The whole visit should prove to be more active and rewarding rather than passive and easily forgotten.

In order to form the habit of using our century books, I found it helpful to make a light comment on how that teaching we had just finished would surely make a good entry. Ordinarily this gentle nudge resulted in the child promptly locating his book and making an entry. To make it easier, the century book needs to be stored in a handy location during school hours so that when the reading and narrating are finished an entry can be made.

Setting the example by keeping your own book can also provide a reminder without the necessity for nagging. I've recently constructed one for myself. My only regret is not keeping one the entire ten years I've home schooled. We have covered so much history during this time because of my own fascination, I know my pages would have been filling up by now.

One Way to Assemble a Century Book

Bernau included in her article detailed and rather complex instructions on how to construct your own book of centuries. The following will serve as example:

"The book consists of forty-eight blank leaves, i.e. ninety-six pages, for drawing, and a corresponding number of lined pages. There are nine double blank pages in the latest 'Book of Centuries,' which can be used for drawings of the ancient gods in the earlier part, and architecture of the period in the later part of the book, or for collections of drawings the owner may wish to make. These nine double-pages come at good intervals, so that they can be used for the Prehistoric Periods, Egyptian (2), Sumerian, Babylonian, Assyrian, Greek or Roman, Saxon, or maps, according to their position in the book. We must start at the beginning of the book and head the first lined page 'Prehistoric Periods.' Under this it is as well to write a list of the chief Periods—Eolithic, Palaeolithic or Old Stone, Neolithic or New Stone, Bronze, and Early Iron—explaining what is meant by each. ...Then we must turn to the twelfth lined page from the end.

Between the two top lines write a large 20th CENTURY, A.D.; from here work backwards, writing at the top of each lined page respectively, 19th CENTURY, A.D., 18th CENTURY, A.D., etc., till the 1st CENTURY, A.D. Continue then from the 1st CENTURY, B.C. till the 54th CENTURY, B.C."

I had to read these directions over and over and over again. After much head scratching I assembled a book following the instructions exactly. I went to the trouble so that others could see the finished product—after all, a picture is worth a thousand words. I have *never* used that book, and I doubt many home schooling parents would. According to Bernau's instructions, the lined paper would have twenty lines on it, each line representing five years, which would equal one hundred years in all. Therefore, the child's notations had to be very brief so as to fit one hundred years' worth on a single sheet. Some examples were provided in her article, and they demonstrated the brevity by including only a name with or without a tiny piece of information. This is far more difficult than it may appear—I suggest you try it yourself before you ask this of the child. Take one sheet of paper and draw twenty lines on it. Then sit down with an encyclopedia and extract some representative events from one century. Because each line is a five year period you can count by five's for easy placement of events. However, you'll quickly see how difficult it is, even when you're being extremely brief, to fit your entries on the lines.

In addition to one lined page the children were allowed one blank sheet per century for illustration. Bernau wrote, "One page is a very small space in which to illustrate a whole century and yet it is a mistake to leave two pages for some centuries . . . as it does away with the whole idea of the book; therefore each should choose what she considers the most characteristic events, planning out the arrangement of the page, as far as possible, before drawing." Bear in mind that, according to Bernau, the hope was that "As the book should be a life-long interest, children had better leave the more difficult subjects till they are old enough to do them justice."

I can understand the strategy behind Miss Bernau's instructions, and, to a point, I can see the value of doing it her way. If you are following these instructions or choose to do so in the future, I would not fault you in the least for it. I am concerned, though, about a ten year old's ability to plan so far ahead and choose "the most characteristic events." What if he makes a childish error or his handwriting is too large to fit within the inch or so provided for a year? I think there is an easier way to explain it, and a more user-friendly way to make these books actually fun and effective.

ANOTHER WAY

Dating the Book

When I designed my less-intense version, I eliminated the suggested sections reserved for "prehistoric periods" specifically listed as Eolithic, Palaeolithic, Neolithic, Bronze and Iron ages by Bernau. If you want to include them then it may help you to know that many Christians recognize the Bronze age to be approximately 3000 B.C. and the Iron age to be approximately 1000 B.C. I didn't go as far back as 104,000 B.C. as was recommended. I'm of the "young earth" persuasion and hold to Christian beliefs so I started our books with 4000 B.C. The age of the earth is a hotly debated point even within the Christian community. Obviously it is up to your discretion. Another way your personal views will impact the century book is when you're at a museum. More often than not the objects displayed will have a written explanation of what it is and the date it is from. When the claim far exceeds the age of the earth itself you can adjust the alleged date and sketch the object where you decide it best fits in your book.

The idea of a museum sketchbook really made an impact on me so I constructed several books from sketch paper. Unfortunately, it was more of a hassle than plain paper. For one thing I couldn't find sketch paper that was already notebook size so I had to cut it myself and then punch three-ring-binder holes in the sides. When I made the book that I'm currently using, I had just received a donation of several very large sheets of quality sketch paper. I took those to a printer and paid to have it cut to 8½x11 inches. They also punched the holes for a very nominal price. I have made century books from computer paper too. It is already the right size and only needs the appropriate holes.

Regardless of what paper you choose you need both blank paper and lined paper. You have the option of using regular lined notebook paper or you can draw twenty lines per sheet using either a computer or pen. I'm glad I used a computer because I can simply open that file and push "print" when I need to make a new book.

Titling the Pages

The easiest way to start, whether by hand or computer, is to write 1st Century A.D. on the top of a lined paper, then write it again on the top of a blank paper. Keep going until you get to the 21st Century. Doing it this way teaches the child that the 20th century encompasses the 1900's. They will then have weekly practice with that concept and will not embarrass themselves in the future. However, I've also made a century books where I titled the centuries A.D. 1800's, A.D. 1900's, etc. This simplification makes it easier for children as they attempt to turn to the right page. The best of both concepts is to label each page by both titles (e.g., 1900's 20th Century) this provides constant reinforcement.

Then you need to title the B.C.'s starting with 100 B.C., then 200 B.C., 300 B.C., and going as far back as your own convictions allow. You can title the B.C.'s using 1st, 2nd, etc. if you wish, but we are not in the habit of referring to them by those names so I recommend naming them by the hundreds. Load these pages into a two inch, three ring binder.

Additional Pages

Another way I veer from Bernau's recommendations is by allowing the addition of as many sheets per century as the child needs or wants.

These can be added in during the initial construction process or later. All centuries do not need additional sheets. Most likely, you'll automatically need more sheets from A.D. 1100 to A.D. 2100. There is a lot of recorded history during this time frame, and many discoveries were (and will be) made. I need to stress that I did not do away with the need for brevity. We only make simple notations such as when Charles Dickens was born or Julius Caesar invaded England.

Additional sheets solve another problem by providing a way for the child to mature with the book. It's supposed to be a lifelong hobby or at least until eighteen years of age. If the child is embarrassed by earlier immature entries, he can stop adding to the sheet and begin using a fresh sheet for that century. I would not let them remove it from the book—they just don't need to add to it if they have run out of room or want to begin a more disciplined version.

What to Enter

For content you could choose a century, cover it and fill in its page. At our house we prefer to keep the book close at hand to use on an "as-needed" basis. Bernau wrote, "Children get accustomed to treating their 'Books of Centuries' as companions *to all their reading.* "This is a very important idea. Most of us tend to compartmentalize our school subjects into language arts (including poetry and literature), religion, math, history and science. So we took "all their reading" to heart at our house. Entries can include the discovery of planets and other scientific breakthroughs. The discovery of a mathematical formula or the birth/death of a mathematician may also find their way into our century books. Biblical events are great additions and help to fill in the B.C. pages. One of my children has sketched Shakespeare on the appropriate page, and when we start or finish a Dickens' book, he likes to note the year that book was written.

Miscellaneous Thoughts

When a child is young I do not make an issue of where on the page the entry is made. As an adult or with a teenager, I would expect some discipline as to where on the page they placed an entry. For example, the re-election of President Clinton would be entered near the bottom of A.D. 1900's.

If you want to be relaxed then forgo the lined sheets and simply title blank sheets by the century to be used for sketching and note taking. One of my children's century book is done that way, and I love it.

It goes without saying that you could assign the child the task of constructing the book if he is old enough and understands what to do.

If money is no object then you can purchase *The Book of the Centuries* that is available wherever home schooling products are sold. Keep in mind when you price these that they can be homemade for a cost of $2.00 to $4.00 depending on the size of the binder and quality of the paper.

OTHER HISTORY IDEAS

Family Century Book

Bernau had another idea of making a family book of centuries. She thought it would help the boarding-school students to be able to participate when they were home for vacation. I referred to this as a good idea in my first book, *A Charlotte Mason Education*. While I still think it could be considered an option, I don't know how one would keep to her exact approach of not allowing more than one page per century without some family squabbles (e.g., little brother's contribution alongside older sibling's painstaking entry). I would allow more pages and have a much looser approach if doing it this way.

United States Century Book

A friend of mine recently mentioned the idea of having a century book dedicated to United States (or any other country) history alone. I'm imagining a half-inch binder with sheets of paper labeled by the decade rather than the century. You could include any map copy work according to decade as the different colony, territory and eventually state boundary lines were established.

Simple Timelines

Keeping a single piece of paper in a history book that serves both as a timeline and a bookmark has been effective for us. Start with a simple line drawn horizontally on the paper and add small vertical lines and a brief notation whenever a significant event occurs. Depending on what you're studying you may find it helpful to draw a line that represents the first century through the twenty–first century to provide context for the time frame the particular events occurred. As the book moves through its material chronologically, mark events on the timeline. For example, if your book is about Benjamin Franklin and it starts with the beginning of his life, your first vertical line and entry will mark his birth at 1706. All other events are noted as they are discussed with the date of his death as a conclusion. Because the timeline is always in the book itself, serving as a bookmark, I see it every time I read from the book, therefore I remember to use it. Usually, when I open the book, I hand the timeline/bookmark to one of the children to review and then do the day's reading. Some days we make an entry and some days there isn't a need for one.

History Charts

Charlotte Mason briefly mentioned history charts on page 177 of *Philosophy of Education*. It is a one-page chart with 100 squares laid out 10x10. These can be made by hand or computer. You can either make it with 100 blank squares or you can add the last two digits of each year in the century (i.e., 00, 01, 02, etc. up to 99) in the corner of each square. These numbers can be made in a very small size so as not to distract from your notations.

The history chart has countless ways it could be used. One idea is to research a century and boil it down to the main events. Perhaps there was a war during the first ten years, a famine in the middle, and a history-making invention, such as the airplane, came into existence during the last half of the century. You would then invent a symbol for war, a symbol for famine and a symbol for the airplane, and place those in the appropriate years. This creates a century at a glance. I may have oversimplified with this example because you could spend a very long time researching the century and spend an equally long time entering the symbols.

I've had an idea of my own concerning these history charts. If you make them on a computer or use a copy machine, you could make a large number at one time and place one adjacent to each century in your century book. Then perhaps you could make entries as you went along, and it would fill in gradually over time like the rest of the book.

Conclusion

Is it possible for a child to fail at keeping a century book? After much thought I've concluded that the only failures might be in either never constructing one in the first place or failing to make it a habit.

No matter how you choose to assemble a century book, it is worth doing. Historical events will begin to appear on the pages and eventually many unrelated people and events will fill in on any given page; that is the exciting part. This gives the child a place to "hang" that information he is getting from all those great books to which he is being exposed. It's personal because the book is his own timeline and the result of his own labor.

Even after years of use there will still be blank pages in the child's book. Either you haven't covered any events that took place in those time frames, or they are the centuries in which not as much history was recorded. That is an interesting fact for a child to discover for himself.

Whichever way you choose to teach history, stop and ask yourself a significant question. Think beyond gaps and even retention of the subject and look to the culmination of all those living books your family will have read. Provide your children with the opportunity to recall each wonderful life they've read about, museum they've visited, and artifact they've drawn as they turn their pages and travel through the centuries.

SEVEN

A Sample Term

A few years ago I was fortunate to come across a wonderful article in Charlotte Mason's *Parents' Review* written in 1922 by Miss O'Ferrall. It described a spring term (a six day school week lasting 66 days) designed for home schooled children who were nine, ten and eleven years old. This group was known as Form II and was divided into two groups that they called A and B. To make this chapter easier to understand I'll call them the older and the younger children. From the article I pulled out exactly what these nine–to eleven–year-old children were responsible for learning in one term, and I've arranged the information in a table format for easy understanding.

This table is tangible proof of the wide education that the home schooled students under Charlotte's direction enjoyed. It should prove to be relatively easy for you to implement the schedule and put the information into practice. Here are a few different ways to use the table or use your imagination to best suit your family.

67

If you have children of this age group, you could set aside a portion of this school year, maybe even the spring, and duplicate exactly what Charlotte's home schooled students did by following the table as closely as possible. It will satisfy your curiosity if you always wanted to know how it was really done then. If your children are not between nine and eleven years old but they are close enough, maybe you can adapt the table accordingly. If they are much younger, I would suggest that you read Charlotte's first volume *Home Education* because it deals with children under nine while it also lays out her entire educational philosophy. If your child is a little older, like twelve or thirteen years old, I still wouldn't hesitate to duplicate this school term; I would just expect better narrations. Another option is to follow the example given (for twelve year olds) in *School Education* (Vol. 3, pages 302–328). First the assignments are detailed, then the exam questions are supplied, and then the answers are also listed as given by a twelve year old. Of course, if all your children are already in high school, this table can simply be an example for you of Charlotte's students' vast exposure to many books and experiences.

It will not be possible to follow it just as it reads because many of the books mentioned are out of print and hard to locate, although some of them are available through interlibrary loans at your local library. This table provides us with a pattern to follow, and many of the subjects will not be affected by out-of-print and hard-to-find books if you find substitute books.

You may not want to put in a loan request on every title discussed here. In fact, I would ask that you don't. In many cases there are only a few copies available in the United States, and if we all were to make requests, we would cause the waiting time to be extended from the already lengthy time to perhaps years. It may be more prudent to order one example from the science section and one from the history section to examine. As we become familiar with a Charlotte Mason-suggested book, we become more equipped to assess materials readily available to us today. As I often mention to people, the Charlotte Mason method does not revolve around a certain book list.

If you live in North America, for example, you'll want to find living books under the categories of history and citizenship that apply to your own country. When it comes time for you to study the European continent, you will still need to find the most interesting books that you can for those countries and not become disheartened if you can't secure these exact titles.

I was fortunate enough to obtain copies of *Our Sea Power, Bulfinch's Mythology, Jack's Insects, Life and Her Children* and *The Sciences*. It took time, money and persistence to locate these books, but I was able to duplicate this term almost exactly. Ideas are included in the appendix on where to look for these and other hard-to-find books.

Obviously, any interesting book that covers Schumann, Julius Caesar and a Longfellow anthology will help you if you're interested in trying to duplicate this term but you don't have to have these exact books in your home. Add a Latin course, singing, keep a century book and some physical education, and you'll be a long way toward emulating this term.

If you can't locate the science books suggested here try a readily available book like Anna Comstock's *Handbook of Nature Study* (ISBN 0-8014-9384-6) or check the book list in the appendix. Another easy-to-find literary science book that might serve as a substitute is *James Heriott's Treasury for Children*. We read the whole thing in a couple of months and loved every second. Don't stop enjoying your nature notebooks, they'll be extremely useful as you work your way through your natural science courses.

For grammar, we can use Charlotte Mason's book *Simply Grammar*, which is the book that was revised by Karen Andreola. This can be used with children from nine to fourteen years old.

Under the subject of drawing, I've tried to find more information about brush-drawing. My most reliable, living Charlotte Mason source concluded that brush-drawing was sketching with a brush rather than a sketch pencil. So you can do just that or pick up some of the Prisma Color Scholar Art Brushes made by Berol. These are a combination of paint brushes and modern-day markers. The order number is PB950;

ask for them where office equipment is sold.

Under the subject of handicrafts, you will see the term Repoussé work. Webster's dictionary defines this as, "shaped or ornamented with patterns in relief made by hammering or pressing on the reverse side—used esp. of metal."

The point is, don't focus on what you can't find—just keep using what you do find. And this is really important: when you find an interesting Charlotte Mason-friendly book, tell all of your friends at your support group.

Please remember and apply the concept of short lessons to this table as well. Also, keep applying the narration process to all those good books that you find. In the original article, O'Ferrall reminded us of the fact that Charlotte Mason's home schooled students participated in end-of-term examinations. Examples of these are supplied in *School Education* (Vol. 3 pgs. 271–299). We too could implement these with our own kids, but please keep this statement of O'Ferrall's in mind, "The examinations are not to be a burden to the children, but a pleasure."

BIBLE
- Exodus 12—Numbers 13:33
- Matt 10—Matt 21:11, I would also include Matt 26 because the last Passover is covered there
- Other Sunday books which were optional—
  Sidelights on the Bible, Wigwam Stories and
  The Northumbrian Saints

ENGLISH HISTORY
- *A History Of England* by Arnold Forster (which covers 55 B.C. to A.D. 910)
- Same time era (55 B.C.-A.D. 910) Of French history from *First History of France* by Mrs. Creighton

CITIZENSHIP
The younger children:
- *Stories from the History of Rome* by Mrs. Beesley
The older children:
- Plutarch's *Julius Caesar*
- *A Citizen Reader* by Arnold Forster

READING
- Shakespeare's *Julius Caesar*
- *The Little Duke*
- *Wigwam Stories*

In Addition the younger children read:
- *The Adventures of Beowulf*
- *The Discoverer of the North Cape*, by Longfellow
- Portions of *The Heroes of Asgard*

In Addition the older children read:
- A period from *Bulfinch's Age of Fable*
- Malory's *The Coming of Arthur*
- *Puck of Pook's Hill*
- Longfellow's *Saga of King Olaf*

GEOGRAPHY
- Portions of Miss Mason's *The Ambleside Geography Books*, book number III (The Counties of England)
- *Our Sea Power*, by H.W. Household
- *Round the Empire*, by Sir George Parkin
- All geography is studied with an Atlas

FRENCH
- Siepmann's Primary French Course
- French Songs, by Violet Partington
- narrations done in French

MATH
The younger children:
- Weights and Measures
- Review
- Practice

The older children:
- Simple Interest
- Compound Practice
- H.C.F. of large numbers

- Practical Geometry

GRAMMAR
- Meiklejohn's *Short English Grammar* (which included parsing and analysis)

NATURAL HISTORY
- *The Sciences*, by E.S. Holden
- Keep a nature diary

The younger children: Either:

- Sections from *Life and Her Children*, by Arabella Buckley,
- or *Jack's Insects*, by Edmund Selous

The older children:
- Sections from *Life and Her Children*, by Arabella Buckley

PICTURE STUDY
- Jan Steen (3 prints)
- Gerard Dou (3 prints)

DRAWING
- six twigs of trees
- studies of animals that the children have been able to watch
- brush-drawing (sketching with a brush rather than a pencil)

RECITATION
- a psalm
- 12 verses from the New Testament
- 12 verses from the Old Testament
- two hymns
- a scene from *Julius Caesar*, or 40 lines from Longfellow

MUSIC
Music Appreciation:
- Schumann
- Piano

SINGING
- two English songs
- two French songs
- sight-singing

DRILL
- Swedish drill
- Ball drill
- Skipping
- etc.

GENERAL HISTORY
Just the older children:
- Reading a book about the British Museum
- Keep their own Century Book

HANDICRAFTS
Boys and Girls both:
- House or garden work
- Repoussé work
- knitting
- sewing
- mend clothes from the wash each week

LATIN
Only the older children take Latin

EIGHT

Curriculum Choosing

*C*hoosing curriculum ranges from a necessary evil to a highly reward-ing task for home schooling families. It also ranges from a complete boxed set of everything you'll ever need to teach your third–grader, to you choosing from among the many thousands of products available.

If you want to strike fear in the heart of any new home schooler just try telling her to "write her own curriculum" as though it's as easy as falling off a log. Drag her along to one of those huge curriculum fairs and watch her melt into a pile of tears and despair. There are so many choices it's no wonder people want help with the actual choosing.

One of the pitfalls of being new to home schooling is that invariably a veteran home schooler will take notice, come alongside and attempt to give her sage advice. This is both good and bad. Of course it can be very helpful, she'll know where the retail outlets for educational materials are located. She'll probably own a crate of home schooling catalogs and be well-versed in all of the shipping rates used by the various companies across the country. The less positive side of a veteran taking you under her wing is she may try to persuade you that her way is the only way.

One very active mentor, such as this, can leave a trail of proselytes in her wake and whether her advice is sound or not make a huge impact on her community. It usually takes a year to get on one's feet no matter what philosophy you first adopt, but adopting an unfruitful philosophy may take an additional year to remedy. A couple of examples would range from an unhappy mom and her unhappy children sitting among a sky-high pile of expensive textbooks because her new friend swears by that approach. Or there's the unfortunate advice of just hanging-out with the children, taking them to the meat counter to learn their mathematics, and getting social studies from afternoon talk shows. You may think I'm exaggerating this point, but I'm not. I've seen these exact examples lived out. The next time someone tells you that her children learn their math at the grocery store effortlessly and that's all the math they'll need, ask her some further questions. Do they pack a calculator or are they going up and down the aisles utilizing mental addition, subtraction, multiplication and division. Maybe one time her children really did glean some math knowledge through osmosis, but I'm alleging it probably was just that—one time.

Another pitfall to avoid is collecting too much curriculum. Some mothers are only happy if UPS rings their doorbell weekly. The excitement of opening new packages is all they know and all they have to hang on to. I've seen this with wealthy and nearly impoverished families alike. It's materialism to the core, but they don't think of it that way because it's for the children's education. The end result is twofold. You can only avoid educating your children for so long and eventually you'll have to own up to the fact that ordering products has served as a distraction from the real work you are to do. The other result is that sooner than you think, you'll have enough inventory to open your own private school.

There are better ways to find the right materials. One of the absolute best solutions is to join, or start, a support group whether it is geared solely to the Charlotte Mason home or open to all home schoolers. (See the question and answer chapter for more ideas.) The key to this is to have a show and tell time either every meeting or semi-annually. One group I participated in took four months of the year (the months before our state convention when everyone stocks up) and concentrated on approximately three subjects per meeting with the intent to have all participants bring the stuff they had used to the meeting. The leader told us to bring things we liked and things we hated. Then we went around the circle and took turns explaining our pile to the group. We practiced the same concept at the Charlotte Mason support group I used to lead. We had our show and tell time at the opening of *every* meeting. It was rewarding for everyone involved to see the great books others had found.

Why is that such a great idea? There is nothing more beneficial than seeing a product with your own eyes. There is simply no substitute for seeing it yourself. Anytime you hear of a hot new product first ask your local home school curriculum seller to order one that you can examine but not be obligated to purchase. Or, if you're patient, wait until your state holds its annual curriculum exhibition and if it's that popular it will be on display there. Some materials have great reputations but that has nothing to do with you, your home and what you like—that's where the product ultimately has to perform. Other people's recommendations are very valuable and not to be ignored, but never, and I mean never, go by someone's recommendation of a product if they have it but have *never* used it!

Another way to view things before buying them is to check with the mom who I affectionately call the "Curriculum Queen." If you have access to a wide enough circle of home schooling parents, you will probably know a woman like this. Every time a certain product comes up in conversation she is the one in the crowd who always says, "I have that!"

Don't forget that you can always make another order. That is the best advice my husband ever gave me when I was new to curriculum choosing. This wisdom only applies to standard curriculum companies that are going to still be in business through the next several millennia. It is highly unlikely that the big businesses are going to stop making that spelling book you think you have to order right now. They might revise it, but that usually consists of a new cover or just enough changes to make the previous answer book obsolete. This does not apply when you're at the antique store and you have in your hand a rare, out-of-print Charlotte Mason jewel. Then your motto should be, "You snooze, you lose."

Don't stock up for the future. Sometimes we think we like something so much that we need to buy one for all the kids who will one day be in that grade level. Don't do it. Good things continue to be created, and you will find new things that you didn't know would be available. You are also prone to become sick of using the same program with more than two or three children.

Perhaps the most important advice I have is this, avoid throwing money at your problems. When we get a little disgruntled with home schooling in general or even a particular child the tendency is to discard what we were using and go shopping again. Now I'm the first to recommend discarding books and materials that are killing the love for learning (no matter what it cost you) but I have seen too many people unable to persevere when it's easier to write a check. This is not usually the best solution to your problem, and there *is* greed in the home schooling market. Many companies are in business to help you by providing the materials you'll need and many view it as a ministry as well as a capitalistic venture. But there are others whose motives are not as noble so do not let them take advantage of you when you're vulnerable.

Because I'm often asked what I use in my home school, I've included a book list in the appendix with my, Charlotte's, and other people who follow the method recommendations all in one place. You'll find a supplies list as well. Here I'd like to include a few curriculum recommendations, that I've used and approve of, primarily concentrating on hands-on products.

I can't say enough about the *Body Book*. It has nothing to do with Charlotte Mason but it is still highly enjoyable and effective for teaching anatomy. The book provides the means for your children to make a life-size human skeleton (from paper), a human eyeball (paper and plastic wrap) and many other projects. The text can be read to the child and narration should be incorporated.

If you use the Body Book it will take several weeks, and I recommend using the buddy system with this book. I invited a good friend and her child over every Wednesday to do the projects with us. That way we finished the course instead of becoming sidetracked and my friend helped by bringing some of the visual aids. The book suggested getting a cross section of a large cow bone from a butcher to show the children. My friend accomplished that task and was the one who willingly displayed it to the kids. That was more than I would have been able to do.

I took the anatomy terms from the book and used them as our spelling words. All the children involved were between third and sixth grade at the time. The sixth grader learned to spell clavicle, mandible, etc. and the third grader learned collar bone, jaw bone, etc. I recommend this book highly because I think it's the best anatomy course for grade school students. The *Body Book* should be available anywhere curriculum is sold.

One summer it became apparent that we had absolutely no geological knowledge in our family. We camped for about four weeks and it seems like everywhere we went we encountered unusual rocks. There was a constant chorus of "Mommy, what's this called?" As is often the case when we're outside I had to answer, "Mommy doesn't know, she went to public school." Shortly afterward I found a really good hands-on, fun to use kit called, *Ring of Fire, Igneous Rocks* by Myrna Martin. The kit includes twelve specimens, a small hand-held microscope and a book. The teaching is clear, the activities are fun and the price is right. As the parent you do not have any additional work such as lesson preparation. The author wrote it to be active learning on the part of the child rather than passive. She expanded the line to include many new kits.

Ordering information is available by writing to: RING OF FIRE, Post Office Box 489, Scio, OR 97374, or E-mail myrnam @teleport.com, or call 888-785-5439.

There are many educational games on the market—some are fun and some are not. I took a chance and bought *The Garden Game*. Fortunately, I was not disappointed. It has an attractive look, well thought out concept, and most importantly it doesn't take long to play. You'll benefit from this if you need to renew your gardening knowledge or your children would like to learn about compost, etc. the fun way. We have played every day since I bought it and we haven't grown tired of it yet, plus it is taking the place of a gardening text for our family. This is available through AMPERSAND PRESS at 750 Lake Street, Port Townsend, WA, 98368 or call 800-624-4263.

Handwriting is a topic I covered in my first book and I don't wish to repeat myself here, but I am often asked which program would best fit with Charlotte Mason's teaching. Remember, most of the practice work of learning both manuscript and cursive writing is done through copy work but I have always recommended and used workbooks for learning letter formation. It is essential unless you want to spend an inordinate amount of time drawing dotted letters for your children to trace. So the question has been which workbook to use until they're ready for transcription.

I have probably used everything on the market in my ten years of home schooling. Nothing really rang my bell until recently I found out about *Cursive Connections*. It is the most well-thought out contribution to handwriting practice books I have ever seen. The layout of the pages proves to be effective for children because they can really look at the letter formation while practicing each and every letter. Children practice letters with similar strokes which greatly helps with learning to link letters together. The results are beautiful letter formation and happy children. Plus, Kathryn Libby's motive for writing the course was to correct the tendency of children to start out with a few good letters only to have them degenerate by the end of the page. The author is currently working on four new cursive courses and I'm hoping she'll publish one for manuscript. You may write to her at: KEL Publications, Post Office Box 260, Gilbert, AZ 85299.

Atlas in a Box: World Geography Card Game is the best educational game we've played, (of course we're easily entertained). All 192 cards represents a country with a map on one side and their flag on the other. Four games are explained in the directions and they include seven other ideas for using the cards. Atlas-in-a-Box is a trademark of Resource Games, Inc., Post Office Box 151 Redmond, WA 98052.

Most home schoolers are already aware of *Rummy Roots and More Rummy Roots*. Our family enjoys these Greek and Latin root word games a lot. Usually children need to be in mid-grade school in order to participate and it will keep their interest through junior high. One of the other language arts is grammar. Having tried nearly everything on the market and never finding anything I liked, I'm still recommending *Simply Grammar*, originally written by Charlotte Mason and now on the market as a revised version by Karen Andreola. Even though it's Charlotte Mason strong opinion that we adults make certain we only give our children one chance at obtaining information and I usually practice that, I don't with this book. I don't announce this to my kids (and they never read my books so they won't know unless you tell them) but each child of mine will go through *Simply Grammar* three separate times with a year or two off in-between. Why do I do this? Because grammar itself is the most forgettable subject. It's complicated and, because you don't need it to talk and write on a daily basis, it does not stay with you. Folks who excel at grammar pursue editing jobs later in life (thank goodness for them) and they are able to help the average person who didn't just step out of a college-level English class.

I'm often asked if *Simply Grammar* will be enough grammar for children. I believe it will be, when used in conjunction with the other language arts techniques written about in *A Charlotte Mason Education*. If your children will go directly into college then I would give them a more strenuous grammar program right before they go. Many of the Rod and Staff English books are strenuous. I have the seventh grade Rod and Staff book and I consider it to be at the collegiate level. Check with your friends, chances are someone will have a grammar book that is extremely difficult. This prepares your children for English 101 but more importantly, it prepares them for college level foreign language.

Frequently, people want to know what reading program or phonics system they should invest in. I have taught almost all of my five children to read—for some it came easy and for others it was a struggle. Once again, there is no substitution for reading directly from C. Mason's six-volume set, and when teaching children to read you want to turn to *Home Education* (Vol. 1) and begin with page 199. She begins her teaching with a description of how the well-known Susana Wesley (mother of twenty–five children) taught her children to read. You should read this for yourself but let me make one comment here, I highly doubt Mrs. Wesley ran out and bought a phonics program that cost her hundreds of dollars.

I found my strategy for teaching children phonics and reading was completely compatible with Charlotte Mason's. (I'd already had some practice with it before I knew her teaching.) In short, the first word we both introduce is "at." By adding different consonants to the front of "at" you get CAT, SAT, MAT, FAT, PAT, HAT, etc. If you keep this philosophy in mind you'll find lots of rhyming words that are spelled the same such as OAT, GOAT, BOAT, MOAT and FLOAT. Sight words need to be acknowledged as such, meaning the child has to memorize the words that do not obey the phonics rules. "Said" and "the" are examples that will "come" right away in the little readers.

Please avoid gimmicks, they just waste your money. Many companies are cashing in on parents' fear. Your purchases can be nominal—not that your children's reading skills are not important to you, of course they are. When I teach reading to the young child the primary thing I need to have is letters. You could make them by hand or computer.

They need to be at least one inch high and there are many ready-made sets on the market. I've used felt and rubber, but paper would work great. A set of capital letters will get you started and if you can add the lower case, so much the better.

I like to practice the alphabet song and the alphabet sounds. A Beka sells a small set of alphabet cards that have all the letters and two cards for each of the vowels. They include a picture on each card so each day (or three times a week) I drill with the child in a "flash card" style. I hold up the "A" card which has a picture of an apple and we say, "A, apple, aaaaa." Make your sound match the beginning vowel in apple. Then I hold up the second "A" card which has picture of an acorn and we say, "A, acorn, aaaaa." We follow with "B, bell, bbbbb," "C, cat, ccccc," "D, door, ddddd." You could make your own set of cards and that way you could include "ah" as in "father." Don't overdo it at first, the schwa, blends, diphthongs and digraphs can wait.

If you know your phonics then the child can do without workbooks because you can teach them as the reading progresses. If you don't know phonics don't feel ashamed, most of us don't when we start home schooling. Buy *one* inexpensive workbook, *not* a box full of doo-dads and tapes unless you have a language barrier yourself. If English is not your native tongue or you have a speech impediment that precludes you from correct pronunciation then you'll want tapes. Again, high price tags are not necessary and should be avoided.

Once you have gone through a workbook with one child you're probably not going to need one ever again. Keep the used one around for reference or do what I did once and take all the teaching in the workbook and write it on one sheet of paper. Next time you can't remember the difference between a blend and a diphthong you can remind yourself quickly. It may take you two children before your phonics knowledge is where you'd like it to be, but if you have more children you'll have plenty of practice and you won't lose that knowledge again.

For first "readers" I like the Fairfax Christian Curriculum Series. I strongly prefer this set over some of the more well known ones but if you have something on hand use it. The Fairfax sets are published by Thoburn Press at Post Office Box 6941, Tyler, TX 75711. Most readers work the same, they begin with short vowel sounds but they have to have some sight words in them. Usually they progress to four letter words with silent "e."

I'm also a fan of the Amish readers and workbooks (if you are looking for a workbook). They're known as the Pathway Readers which can be ordered directly from the Amish and many catalog companies carry them. I bought all the readers, the primer through eighth grade, I no longer recommend that. Charlotte Mason families would much rather get out of the reader as soon as possible and into real books, whole books and the great literature. Instead, I think you'll be happy getting the first two or three of the set. Pathway sells a set of flash cards that goes with their readers. If you want to duplicate *Home Education's* teaching without cutting apart books or making your own words then buy the flash cards. I've found that children who learn to read quickly and effortlessly will not need the flash cards. I've also found that children who find learning to read a big challenge greatly benefit from the cards. You may write to Pathway at: Pathway Bookstore, Route 4 Box 267, LaGrange, IN 46761.

The rest of the language arts can be nearly free of charge. I haven't spent any money on language arts for over four years. I accomplished that by following Charlotte Mason's advice which I wrote about in *A Charlotte Mason Education.*

You'll find some of my math ideas in the question and answer chapter and I will end this segment by pointing out that new materials are constantly being introduced. Many catalog companies review products and there are entire books available whose sole objective is to review. My small consolidation of suggestions does not do the market justice. Keep an open mind and a fairly closed checkbook and you will find many worthwhile materials.

NINE

High school

$\mathcal{M}$any parents lose their confidence to home educate when their children approach the junior and senior high years. There are many factors to consider such as graduation, college entrance and job preparation.

Formerly, we counted seat work hours and when a child had reached 180 sessions, consisting of 50 minutes each, we granted the student one credit. The United States is in the process of replacing credits (which used to be recorded on transcripts) with examinations to determine whether the subject has been mastered.

Again, I do not claim to know how that change will effect each family. The country may abandon it and return to counting credits. The primary concern for the home schooling parent is to know the law and the lawmakers in our respective states. For your own protection and the protection of others you should consider joining Home School Legal Defense Association. At the time of this writing they have over 55,000 members and a staff of over 50 people. In exchange for an annual membership fee those who join receive free legal help in the area of home schooling, should they ever need it. Their address is Post Office Box 3000, Purcellvill, VA, 20134.

Completely within our control is our educational philosophy. This is no time to lose sight of the purpose of education. As discussed in the liberal education chapter the goal is not merely to have our young people prepared for the work force. As you contemplate the purpose of secondary education let's look at this very reassuring comment of Charlotte Mason. "But the function of education is not to give technical skill but to develop a person; the more of a person, the better the work of whatever kind;" (Vol. 6, p. 147) The key is to focus on what *kind* of a person we are raising instead of concentrating solely on labor skills or entrance examinations. We need to know what our priorities really are before we'll be able to achieve them.

One popular goal for many home educating families (including my own) is the ability to think well. Everybody wants their adult children to be able to think. Future professors, employers and spouses will appreciate this skill too. Charlotte Mason wrote, "People are naturally divided into those who read and think and those who do not read or think; and the business of schools is to see that all their scholars shall belong to the former class;" (Vol. 6, p. 31)

In Jenny King's book *Charlotte Mason Reviewed*, she writes, "A teacher was once asked, 'What do you teach?' Came the answer: 'I try to teach the children to think.' 'That,' said the questioner, 'is the most important thing to do.' Charlotte Mason's philosophy put into practice in the classroom will do just that and more—a delight in knowing, a search for truth and a love of beauty. What better way of fitting the children for life not only in the twenty-first century, but also the last decades of the twentieth." (p. 60)

I agree wholeheartedly with King that C. Mason's methods will take us into the twenty-first century and as I've looked around at other educational philosophies I have not found any of them to be superior in the area of thinking. Many home schooling families are targeting this goal and it is one of the goals in classical education. It has become increasingly common to combine a classical education with a Charlotte Mason education. Some are using Charlotte's method in the grade school years with the determination to switch to classical education in the older grades. Both are valid choices and I've always stood for individual freedom to make Charlotte Mason's methods work *for* you, on your terms, but I see one common mistake being made by many of those who intend to start with Charlotte Mason and switch to classical in high school. Due to the popularity of classical education there is much to read and that is my suggestion—read as much as you can. I've read several different author's teachings on classical education and I noticed a crucial progression involving three stages. The grammar (elementary grades), the logic (junior high grades), and the rhetoric stage (high school). Evidently, every subject has a grammar so we are not talking about grammar as only an element of language arts. So in the grammar stage of a classical education the goal is to instill facts, many facts, that will be built upon during the later stages. If you skip that step those facts will not be there to serve the child in junior and senior high. Therefore, it's important to be aware of the methodology of classical education so that you don't find yourself with an unforeseen problem.

This brings us to what I see as the two primary differences between the methods. Charlotte Mason made herself clear about her convictions that children are not receptacles into which we pour facts. Perhaps, more importantly, Charlotte Mason had a huge concern that the children would develop a love for learning that adults did not kill. This love would hopefully carry on into adulthood and stay with the individual for life. The fast track, in my opinion, to killing the love of learning is boredom—to me, they are opposites. Mason accused the educationalists of the 1840's and 1850's of forgetting about, "the immense capacity for being bored which is common to us all, and is far more strongly developed in children than in grown-up people. The objects which bore us, or the persons who bore us, appear to wear a bald place in the mind, and thought turns from them with sick aversion." (Vol. 1, p. 263)

Charlotte strongly urges teachers to lean toward knowledge and ideas rather than compiling as many facts as possible. She wrote a letter to some children in which she said "I think that is a joyful thing to be said about anybody, that he loves knowledge; there are so many interesting and delightful things to be known that the person who loves knowledge cannot very well be dull." (WES Pamphlet)

Another point I have in defense of the Charlotte Mason method is its use and continuous practice of narration. Narration involves the ability to communicate but it is not merely parroting. Essex Cholmondeley when writing on narration said, "The mind at work has a threefold activity. It attends; it reflects; it uses what has been apprehended." She went on to write, "Between attention and expression lies a whole world of thought . . . " Everybody has the potential to put forth an opinion logically and defend it under scrutiny, narration provides the practice necessary for that and I believe it equates to the rhetoric stage of the trivium as used in classical education and in the liberal arts.

It is not my wish to offend the many parents, schools and others involved with combining these two methods. I applaud the return to literature in both methods and the many other great attributes they each have. I find the suggested reading lists of those in classical education to include the highest level writing mankind has ever produced and who wouldn't admire and respect those capable of comprehending that most difficult reading. My concern is that you make your decisions as fully informed as possible because those high school years pass quickly. My favorite written work on classical education is co-authored by Douglas Wilson, Wesley Callihan and Douglas Jones and is entitled *Classical Education & The Home School*, published by Canon Press, Moscow,

Idaho. Another excellently written book is *Classical Education—Towards the Revival of American Schooling* by Veith and Kern.

Knowledge itself is another leading goal for secondary school. If we're looking for knowledge that "yields us lifelong joy and contentment" we need to watch our motives. We desire children who seek knowledge for its own sake and "not for the sake of showing off, and not for the sake of excelling others . . . " (Vol. 4, p. 78)

In the high school years it's tempting to revert back to information "cramming" that has been so popular for so very long but does not aid in the retention of knowledge. To prove my point I'd like to tell you about the hardest anatomy instructor in all the world. She taught the most grueling course I ever had in college—I decided to fight all the odds and go for the "A." Sure, there was a textbook, but she liked to lecture, very quickly I might add. Every Friday there was a test and the material came from notes only available from her lectures. Every Friday I got an "A" and every Monday I'd think about the last test. I knew I would never pass it if it were given to me a second time without warning, let alone get a good grade. Is that knowledge? Would you want me to be your physician? Probably not and that's why I think knowledge is the opposite of cramming.

Instead of shoving as much information into the young adult's mind as we possibly can, we could set a whole new goal. I am talking about improved personal traits such as magnanimity as demonstrated in this Charlotte Mason quote. "Upon the knowledge of these great matters — History, Literature, Nature, Science, Art—the Mind feeds and grows. It assimilates such knowledge as the body assimilates food, and the person becomes what is called magnanimous, that is, a person of great mind, wide interests, incapable of occupying himself much about petty, personal matters. What a pity to lose sight of such a possibility for the sake of miserable scraps of information about persons and things that have little connection with one another and little connection with ourselves!" (Vol. 4, p. 78)

Regardless of the direction my children may choose for their own occupations whether it be from the blue collar fields, the various professions or homemaking, I want the above quote to describe them when they are adults. In short, an education based on knowledge is a superior education.

My third goal for high school students is the development of good habits. I have good news and bad news regarding habits. First, all of those good habits you targeted and helped to establish when the children were still in the elementary grades are going to be there for you now, *when you need them the most.* Charlotte Mason thought much of well-brought-up people and even said, "The well-brought-up child has always been a child carefully trained in good habits." However, you're not finished training your children because these last few academic years are basically your final opportunity to instill any habits that you are interested in them displaying as adults.

Whether your children are college bound or not, good study habits will benefit them. As will the ability to arrive places on time and to complete goals in a timely way. Chronic tardiness is a bad habit and I believe we would agree that procrastination is also habitual. I could attempt to give you a list of good and bad habits but I do not think my list will have the desired effect that your own list will have on your students. As the high school years approach, I suggest that you give some serious thought to your teenage children's habits and continue to apply the Charlotte Mason principles, foremost of which is tackling one habit at a time.

Yet another goal to be considered is Charlotte Mason's concept of teaching ideas rather than facts. Mason wrote that ideas are the food of life. "We feed [the children] upon the white ashes out of which the last spark of the fire of original thought has long since died. We give them second-rate story books, with stale phrases, stale situations, shreds of other peoples thoughts, stalest of stale sentiments." (Vol. 3, p.121) The obvious key word there was *stale.* Many parents approaching the high school years see this as a time to "crack down" and abandon all of that "living education" stuff. Their solution usually includes a pile (or two) of ugly, boring, stale, textbooks containing what they believe the child will "need." But remember whether a person is six or one-hundred-six they will learn and retain more if the material is interesting.

According to Jenny King, classroom lecture does not foster the gaining of ideas because the "human mind must be given time to read, mark, learn and inwardly digest before there is any sign of understanding and this can only be tested by the pupil himself relating what he knows . . . give the children living ideas in well-written books and they will grapple with the contents and make them their own." (*Charlotte Mason Reviewed*, p. 29)

The teaching of ideas continues to be one of the key Charlotte Mason strategies. This begins in grade school and is continued throughout the education process, if not life itself. I have found as the parent that I can see evidence on the face of a child when an idea is being grasped.

The previous writing was an attempt to define ideas and deal with how we might introduce them to children but I have even more good news about working with the junior and senior high students. In the later school years our children's minds have matured and developed. Mentally working with an idea should be even more fruitful of an experience than with the child of eight or nine. The love for learning we held to as such a vital Charlotte Mason teaching when the kids were young still applies. My point is that if boredom and love for learning are opposite concepts (and I believe they are) this is not the time to return to standby materials.

The last goal is being well read. Many, many, decades ago to be well read was synonymous with being well educated. Chalk it up to living in a television, motion picture, video society or perhaps there are other pastimes that interfere by competing for the time necessary to read. King wrote in 1981, "Charlotte Mason would have been saddened to see so many children unable to express themselves in good clear language which can only be achieved by *reading or being read to*. Language is a very important aspect of society and a part of culture which is sadly neglected." (*Charlotte Mason Reviewed*, p. 14)

You're probably aware of the large quantity of reading aloud that Charlotte Mason parents do for their children. You may also be aware that Netta Franklin wrote, "We want to counteract slipshod style and bad taste in reading, writing, and speaking, we shall not lightly abandon this custom of reading aloud to children, even when they are grown boys and girls." So the reading aloud can go right on into high school but the good news is many of those short, oral readings you were responsible for, can for the most part, be replaced by longer, silent reading sessions that the children are able to do on their own. This is a huge step toward the goal of self education.

The fact that you tried to develop good literary taste in your child can really bear some fruit in your young adult. Perhaps more important than that is the concept Charlotte often refers to as "read to know." That is the bright side, my friend, a child who can, at long last, read to know.

Dr. Beechick, a well-known home school author, recently wrote that the foremost thing a high school-aged child needs in order to get into college is to have a high reading ability. Her example was if a child "knows a lot of biology and can think critically in that subject, he can read about a less familiar subject, say botany or chemistry."

Being well read does involve careful selection of reading materials. Poetry, classics and literature (rather than textbooks) are great choices. Panicking is not the solution to your high school doubts and neither is resorting to textbooks out of fear. Some think literature and whole books are for little children and as far as older children are concerned it's time to grow up and learn to work in a textbook. Well, I'm not entirely against textbooks, but I can tell you about their origin. While I researched the liberal arts as written about in another chapter I found something unexpected. When it was decided that the uneducated couldn't possibly understand the liberal arts and the practical arts were invented to solve the problem, guess what—they also assumed that "class" of people could not understand whole books written by authors so they created the textbook.

Please realize that it is not my desire to offend my fellow home schooling parents. I think teaching from textbooks (with a Charlotte Mason ribbon tied around it) is one of many valid options. You'll find some children and adults strongly prefer textbook studying to the whole book method.

When I'm asked what a parent is to do with a child like that, I answer from experience. One of my five had a strong preference for textbooks. I let her approach her studies in the way she was leaning toward. My observation of textbooks is that there is a lack of retention, but, if the student likes textbooks, and has retention, then I advise the parent to relent. Because you know your child better than anyone else, I urge you to combine various methods until your child is happy with her own approach to home education.

Fear often sends folks running back toward textbooks and as you may already know Charlotte did not think highly of them. She wanted our books to "be of a literary character," If you've ever wondered if she softened her opinion or eventually found that textbooks had improved, here's your answer. Within the last months of her life she gave her last address before the PNEU In 1922, at 80 years old and after an entire life spent working with children she said, "Therefore the current textbooks of the classroom must be scrapped and replaced by literature, that is, by books into the writing of which the writer has put his heart, as well as a highly trained mind."

Dr. Beechick gave us an excellent summary to the textbook dilemma with this well written statement, "it is impossible to study everything that a group of people would list as essential. Textbooks try to do that, but they sacrifice much depth and interest and thinking in order to skim over numerous topics."

Let's take a close look at several other Charlotte Mason techniques and evaluate each in the light of high school. Variety is a priority for elementary-aged children and it continues to be important in secondary school. To achieve it, one needs fresh books. The best choice is the advanced, interesting literature. Another crucial aspect of variety is to continue to provide a wide range of materials. There is no need to abandon art appreciation, poetry, music, science, math, history or the book of centuries. Techniques that brought refreshment to you and the children will continue to do so.

Another Charlotte Mason technique you'll want to maintain is narration. It is one of the most crucial teachings of Charlotte's and it needs to be incorporated as much as possible. The young adult needs practice with both oral and written narration as the ability to express oneself, put forth an opinion and defend it is needed both in college and in adult life.

Narration, both orally and in the written style, should be practiced constantly. Improving upon the high school child's ability to orally narrate helps in the area of public speaking about which Charlotte wrote that children "read with absolute attention and that, having read, they *know*. They will welcome the preparation for public speaking, an effort for which everyone must qualify in these days, which the act of narration offers." (Vol. 6, p. 124)

Written narrations are the best preparation for essay writing. One of my children has been through a couple years of community college and even though our society is at an all time low point academically they still used essay writing, in fact it was a frequent assignment and often used in place of a test. Narration is the best test of what a person knows. The concept that you can only narrate what you do know, you cannot narrate what you do not know applies at the high school level as much, if not more, as the primary level.

Yet another activity advocated by Mason is being outside everyday. This was one of the most highly emphasized teachings in *Home Education*. Admittedly that book was written to the parents of younger children but I have given this a lot of thought. Why not continue the habit of getting those children outside on a constant basis even during the high school years? It appears to me, that children between the ages of thirteen and nineteen need to be outside more than ever in their lives. Children *can* become moody and confused during these years and seem to greatly benefit from fresh air, hiking and beautiful scenery.

According to the Mason's philosophy one of the objectives in nature study and being outside is to see the Creator in the created and to sense our own insignificance. I have witnessed transformations occur and perspective gained from outdoor activities both in my own life as a teen and in the lives of my children.

In addition, the students attending Charlotte Mason's college were required to take nature walks and keep a nature diary. The college also had a botanical garden where the "idea was to arrange little flower beds round a central point, each demonstrating a major botanical family." (*Charlotte Mason College*, p. 20)

Perhaps lots of outdoor time will help your children to better educate the following generation whether in a classroom or with their own offspring should they decide to home educate. Not only will they be more knowledgeable about plants, animal and bird identification but it's time to recognize that modern civilization has been educating indoors for too long. Young people are kept inside for the majority of the day, they even swim indoors. There was a time when people lived in more of an agrarian culture and when someone went on to a university setting it followed years of outdoor living. That's a different perspective than we currently have.

Charlotte Mason wrote about many other things that continue to apply to the older child. She wrote a great deal about authority. What teenage child has not struggled with that? You'll find her book *Ourselves* (Vol. 4) and *Formation of Character* (Vol. 5) to be good places to read about many moral training issues. I concluded that the subject of authority was the central theme of *School Education* (Vol. 3). If we want teachable children (and who doesn't?) it helps to establish the fact that teachers and parents are also under authority. The key is for the child to recognize that authority is as "universal and as inevitable" as gravity. (Vol. 3, p. 126)

In the Charlotte Mason method we always try to introduce the concrete before the abstract in areas such as math and science. In both of these subjects we attempt to introduce the thing before we present the name of the thing. We attempt to show math concepts with real objects before we teach the abstract manipulation of numbers as symbols. This works regardless of a person's age. In fact it may prevent the, "When am I ever to need this?" protesting that is so common in high school.

Masterly inactivity is yet another concept many probably have trouble implementing or even understanding. It comes naturally to adults to meddle in a child's affairs. It's also too easy to make false assumptions about their intelligence and underestimate their abilities. This is important because when we think the child incapable, something within us wants to do too much for him. The goal is self education about which Charlotte Mason wrote, "I should like to dwell on the enormous relief to teachers, a self-sacrificing and greatly overburdened class." (Vol. 6, p. 32) Thank goodness someone noticed, I do feel a little overburdened occasionally.

On page 6 of *Philosophy of Education* is an outline from which I'd like to print only the first two points:

a) The children, not the teachers, are the responsible persons;
   they do the work by self-effort.

b) The teachers give sympathy and occasionally sum up but the
   actual work is done by the scholars.

Masterly inactivity can be applied academically and as a parenting tool. It's the balanced place between over protection and way too much freedom. Do take notice that the inactivity on your part is supposed to be "masterly." Plain inactivity is not the goal, in fact, it could be called neglect. The adult needs to involve herself when necessary. As King wrote, "Children will make mistakes, they will misbehave in all manner of ways. This is the natural way to grow up. The child who is too securely guarded against his mistakes has little chance of learning by experience." Charlotte Mason offers much information on this topic in *School Education*, Vol. 3 pgs. 25 through 35.

Charlotte Mason strongly preferred to call her teachings an educational method, not a system. Charlotte did not want a rigid system which she said "has an infinity of rules and instructions as to what you are to do and how you are to do it." (Vol. 2, p. 168) When she referred to her philosophy she said "We have a method of education it is true, but method is no more than a way to an end, and is free, yielding, adaptive as Nature herself."

So the question is, what method do we want to use for junior and senior high school? If we've been using Charlotte Mason's ideas successfully with young children do we need to change our method because they matured? Are we going to change our purpose? Do we want a new direction? I invite you to examine each Charlotte Mason technique for yourself and decide one by one which, if any, need to be discarded.

When I did this I did not find any discards—I'm more than content to continue as before. If a child has been in the Charlotte Mason method throughout his lifetime he should be ready to continue in the same manner with more success simply due to his maturation if nothing else.

Only you can answer these questions and only you can determine *if* you are apprehensive about high school and if so *why*.

Some of the universal concerns seem to be:

1. How to teach at that age level (Is Mason's method appropriate for high school?)
2. What to teach at that age level (Can I present sufficient materials?)
3. Fear of teaching that age level (Will I be sufficient?)

It's clear to me that we are talking about at least two different things. *How* you teach and *what* you teach are two different things. The question that has been asked on a nationwide level is, "How do we use the Charlotte Mason method in high school?" My answer is the methodology remains the same although the child has matured (thank heaven) and is now more capable of enjoying, comprehending and expressing himself about all this adult level material that he has always had access to in the past. Some of the confusion seems to come from that fact that there isn't any higher level material to turn to after using adult level material. In other words we've already introduced adult level literature, noble poetry, an appreciation of the fine arts, etc. that many other educational methods would have put off until the high school years. Because there is nothing higher than adult level some are left asking where do we go from here.

However, before we go any further I'd like to address fear. Many parents fear the high school material itself. If fear is really the problem and you question whether you can teach at those grade levels, ask yourself why. Is the fear arising from memories of high school, perhaps one particular academic area such as algebra. Maybe you feel as though you never conquered some of the sciences, maybe no one knows you got a "D" in chemistry. When my oldest child was still in grade school I wondered about many of these things myself.

How about the "Mount Everest" of all home schooling fears, gaps. You and I both graduated with gaps in our education, they are absolutely inevitable. There is not a person alive who does not have gaps. The best way to alleviate this fear is to be realistic about it by first recognizing the unavoidable truth. If you try too hard to cover everything the results usually are a hazy recollection, not true knowledge.

Three things helped me to put aside fear and face high school. First, I visited the local high school my oldest daughter would have attended. Secondly, now that I'm the teacher, I'm in possession of the answer book. (They didn't trust me with one of those when I was the student.) Lastly, I matured. So many subjects literally scared me when I was the teenager. As an adult the more high school curriculum I looked at the better I felt. The turning point came when I looked at a well-known company's Physics book and thought it looked easy. I guess watching public television (and a little Jeopardy) coupled with maturity have given me an edge I didn't have when I was fifteen years old.

Once the Charlotte Mason method is understood and being implemented by any given individual their attention always turns to "what should I be covering?" Many parents want exact information about what to cover. Not surprisingly, when you know Charlotte Mason, she does not provide a comprehensive scope and sequence of each grade for us to follow. Perhaps that would have fallen under the category of "system" she wished to avoid. She does recommend book titles among her written work and I've attempted to extract those into a list provided in the appendix.

One of the sources I've found that details "what" her older students studied is in the back of *School Education* (Vol. 3). Much can be learned about the twelve-year-old's curriculum by reading from page 300 to nearly the end of the book. The books they read from are listed and the examination questions and answers are provided. It is impressive!

Part of the examination described in volume three is to write twenty lines on "An Autumn Evening" in the metre of *The Lady of the Lake*. In our home we have read from this 243 page poem written by Sir Walter Scott but I never would have thought of asking my twelve year old (and I did have one at the time) to emulate the style. One particular child's examination is made available to us and the complete "programme" printed for us which included the material that was covered during the sixty–six day term. The subjects covered included four foreign languages and English grammar.

The students studied three countries for history, (English, French and Roman). They memorized three poems and text from their Bible lesson book. Other subjects listed are dictation, singing, geography, drawing, natural history, botany, physiology, arithmetic, Euclid and geometry. They did not neglect reading, composition, gardening or physical education. The handicrafts included bent iron work, crochet, needlepoint, and they made a linen book cover completely self-designed and constructed.

When the Charlotte Mason students were between eleven and twelve through the age of fifteen they were referred to as class III. In our day high school freshmen are fourteen and the sophomores are usually fifteen so when you read the following list imagine the early high school curriculum and see if you can glean a subject list applicable to your students. "Bible Lessons and Recitations (Poetry and Bible passages); English Grammar, French, German, and Latin; Italian (optional); English, French, and Ancient History (Plutarch's Lives); Singing (French, English, and German Songs); Writing, Dictation, Drill; Drawing in Brush and Charcoal; Natural History, Botany, Physiology, Geography; Arithmetic; Geometry, and Reading. About thirty–five books are used." (Vol. 3, p 286) The time per day was three and a half hours with one–half hour donated to exercise and games. This age group is required to write all of their answers during end of term examinations.

It is my opinion that these insights could be applied to our home schools today. I also believe you and your children could be kept pretty busy trying to follow in the footsteps of the Charlotte Mason students. I would be pleased to even get close. With a few substitutions, we can provide a great education to our children using the above as our curriculum.

Okay, now we all want to know "what" class IV covered don't we? Before we get into the few details provided in the six-volume set let's tackle the statement made on page 294 of *School Education*. "Girls are usually in Class IV for two or three years, from fourteen or fifteen to seventeen, after which they are ready to specialise and usually do well."

It may be the above quote or perhaps others that have sprouted the rumor that the Charlotte Mason method is for girls and not for boys. I am in no way an expert on each and every nuance of English society particularly during Charlotte Mason's time. Yet, by combining this insight with some things she wrote in the sixth volume it becomes evident that the secondary schools of her time were working toward the goal of passing the examinations given prior to admittance to universities. She thought that the primary school-aged children were given a more liberal education and that it produced "more intelligence and wider knowledge" than older children in preparatory school. She noted that there were exceptions in Latin and math.

So I do not think we should hold it against Charlotte Mason, or her examples, that the boys were possibly not available during the late high school years. It is clear to me she would have gladly retained them and offered them the same quality of materials she had always believed in. In fact she also wrote about the boys' preparatory schools of the secondary level that were enrolled in her Parents' Union Schools in *A Liberal Education for All*, "These schools are seriously handicapped by the necessity of fitting their pupils for the Entrance Examinations of Public Schools. Headmasters would find that the History, Literature, Science and Art Work of a School in which no preparation is required and knowledge is ensured would secure a sound foundation in these subjects without encroaching on the time already given to classical and mathematical work." (p. 12)

I think we face a similar dilemma today when we cover vital subjects that are never tested or acknowledged by standardized tests. It's not that I want my children tested on the humanities, that would really take the fun out of it, I'm speaking to the time and effort spent in literature and the arts that no one ever seems to care about. I suppose we have to derive satisfaction from within ourselves that we've covered a great variety and retained much knowledge on our subjects.

Some of "what" class IV studied included the addition of "Geology and Astronomy to the sciences studied, more advanced Algebra to the Mathematics and sets the history of Modern Europe instead of French history. The literature, to illustrate the history, includes the reading of a good many books, and the German and French books when possible illustrate the history studied. All the books (about forty) are of a different calibre from those used in the lower classes; they are books for intelligent students." (Vol. 3, p. 294) Not only did the caliber of reading increase for this class, so did the expectations during written narrations and examinations as written about on page 193 of volume six.

Now that we've checked on Charlotte's curriculum as best as we could, we can look at "what" I taught my former high school student. When my (now adult) daughter was approaching ninth grade I went to my local high school guidance counselor's office and requested a copy of their scope and sequence. It detailed on one sheet of paper everything the children in my city would cover during the last four years (grades nine through twelve). When they would cover algebra, history, science, etc. and what they would cover was all in one place for me to refer to easily. (I have requested these scope and sequences at my local grade school and junior high as well.) At the time, I was experienced with the Charlotte Mason method and was practicing it regularly in my home school so I made the decision to teach *what* the local high school taught only I did it *my* way and I included C. Mason subject matter that the high school was not going to cover. Again, I'm stressing the point that what you teach and how you teach are two different things.

You could do the same as I did or there are other ways to accomplish the same thing. One option is to copy the Charlotte Mason curriculum as closely as you can, or perhaps combine it with the subjects usually covered in your area if it will better prepare your students for college classes or the work force. Look at the home school catalogs, specifically at the high school materials and you'll find a pattern there. Most of the textbooks and other materials are covering roughly the same information during (approximately, if not exactly) the same grades. Also check with several private schools and you'll soon get an idea of what every other high school student in our country is studying.

Now the trick is to get the very best materials. It has always been the task of the Charlotte Mason devotee to find interesting books and it always will be. No doubt someone, sometime will write a curriculum and if you find yourself in agreement with it then you'll be spared this task, but until that time it is up to you and completely within your discretion.

I have always been happy to have the privilege to choose my materials and I've never really desired to have anyone else tell me what to use—although I'm elated when someone else makes a good recommendation. So in my independence I've made the decision that for my family the high school years are reserved for some of the more difficult material such as the Greek and Roman mythology. I have no problem waiting until then to cover things of that nature due to my religious beliefs. To me it's important to ground the children on Biblical precepts and after they have thorough knowledge in that field *then* they can better interpret the gods represented in mythology.

Similarly in Shakespeare's works I read plenty of his plays to my younger children but I reserved many more of them for the late teen years. I found it very fulfilling to watch my former high school student go through plays such as Romeo and Juliet at a time when her intellect had greatly matured and she was able to write the highest quality narrations I've yet to see. Another way we enjoyed Shakespeare together was by obtaining two copies of the same play and reading them aloud together. I know it sounds sappy, but we both really liked it. There are a great number of characters in many of the scenes so we would decide ahead of time whose lines I would read and whose she would read. She would do this every chance she got.

Foreign language is another area where some true advancement can occur. If you followed Charlotte's advice of starting young then the high school years should bear the fruit of the earlier labor resulting in the mastering of a second language.

Any of the fine arts such as the masterpieces of the great artists, the composers and the poets are grasped by the young adult mind with more maturity than a grade school student and this again brings a lot of fulfillment to you as the parent who has gone to the effort to present the humanities.

Starting the Charlotte Mason Method with Older Children

If you happen to be starting your home school efforts with older children then I can think of absolutely nothing in Charlotte's teachings that you should avoid or disregard. You who find yourself in this circumstance will have to go through the transition process with your child in many areas as they adapt from previous educational methods to the Charlotte Mason ideas. I would advise you to be as patient as possible. Charlotte wrote that "Teachers err out of their exceeding good will and generous zeal. They feel that they cannot do too much for children and attempt to do for them those things which they are richly endowed to do for themselves." (Vol. 6, p. 190) Well, no more of that, it's high time we let them exercise their minds, we just need to let them. As G. F. Husband wrote, "The less the teacher talks, the more the class will have to think."

An older child will have to learn to narrate just like a younger child would. I would start with letting this student read a passage and then retell it to you in his own words. Keep in mind, this comes easier to some. Increase the amount of reading material he is responsible for as soon as possible. After he seems to have mastered verbal narration have him try written narration. You're going to have to be consistent, it's the only way he'll progress with this skill.

I was recently asked if older children move pass simple retelling to the stages of analyzing, conclusions, opinions, comparisons, etc. I think it comes naturally. To be able to retell without bias is something a lot of people don't know how to do. I think that's what makes a good researcher. You need to get the facts from a variety of sources and then add your opinions if necessary.

I'm frequently asked if questioning children is better than having them narrate. G. F. Husband wrote, "We of the P. U. S. [Mason's Parents' Union Schools] say: Let the child himself do that which the teacher usually does for him. Let the child by narration supply both the question and answer."

One thing you might encounter with a child in transition is the attitude problem pubescent children sometimes exhibit. If your children have gotten by with very little effort through the inane process of answering the end of chapter summary questions, or "fill in the blank" using the list of words provided, or multiple choice, then they are going to find simple techniques such as paying attention and narration take work. But as we follow Mason's philosophies, we need to remember our goals—one of them being the goal of knowledge not merely the passing of tests. Charlotte has said many times and in many ways that knowledge is not assimilated until it is reproduced and she also asserted that paying attention is a natural function of the brain and does not bring about fatigue if applied correctly.

I believe that we currently have a generation where many teenagers possess brains that have had too much fallow time. Just like with fallow ground, we need to till, prepare earth, plant and fertilize. In the most extreme cases you may have to do more than cultivate the soil—you may need to deforest first. According to most veteran home schooling parents, that project has been known to take up to a year. I'm referring to simultaneously deprogramming and becoming reacquainted. Once the initial work is accomplished then, as with a good gardener, the parent would be able to fall back to simple maintenance.

Do not let your adolescent children manipulate you into believing the Charlotte Mason method is worthless, non-beneficial or dated. Most who know her work and beliefs agree that her techniques and advice are not only ahead of her time but that they are timeless. In other words they can and should be applied to even the most "high tech" material of the 21st century.

If the transition process proves to be exasperating, don't give up. Children are born to test the limits and we all know raising them can be very trying. I'm not going to lie to you and promise that you will have beautiful carefree days. I like to be realistic when I teach people about home schooling. I only have three strategies that I can suggest. Patience, perseverance and discipline. Remember, don't let your decisions be ruled by fear.

The child new to home schooling should be introduced to good books, art and music including Shakespeare and poetry. Charlotte wrote about higher education saying it "may be effected more readily by Milton, Gibbon, Shakespeare, Bacon, and a multitude of great thinkers who are therefore great writers." (Vol. 6, p. 124) Don't be afraid to challenge their minds. As Charlotte wrote, "We owe it to children to let them dig their knowledge, of whatever subject, for themselves out of the fit book; and this for two reasons: what a child digs for is his own possession; what is poured into his ear, like the idle song of a pleasant singer, floats out lightly as it came in, and is rarely assimilated."(Vol. 3, p. 177)

If a child has been in the C. Mason method all along he should be ready to continue in the same manner with more success due to his maturation. After all, we have led them to self education and now we get to "cash in" on our efforts.

I have been asked if I thought the Charlotte Mason method would prepare children for college. My impression on this topic is that Charlotte Mason children have had a superior education and have learned to read information and assimilate it quickly and accurately. This is important to educated professionals such as lawyers, counselors and physicians. As Charlotte wrote, "Contrast this with the wandering eye and random replies of the uneducated;—and you will see that to differentiate people according to their power of attention is to employ a legitimate test." (Vol. 1, p. 137) They are able to think and react to new information, which is something that would be helpful at most college campuses.

Charlotte Mason children have had regular practice with the essay process through the art of narration. They are already accustomed to clearly stating their comprehension on any subject matter.

The other consideration is preparing your children for the examinations, both to enter college and the ones to be given during classes. Charlotte Mason had an opinion on this; she noted that undue importance was placed on one's mathematical skills because it is exceedingly easy to test for. Every answer is either right or it is wrong. She questioned the exclusion of some people from college simply based upon their math scores. However, she had to live with the established conditions of her day so she had her students prepare especially for entrance examinations—and so should we. After they have received a well-rounded education from you and have chosen a direction for their life, then I feel our duty is to help them to succeed.

When my oldest daughter reached high school she went to the library to check out test preparation books (such as the one specifically designed for the SAT®). She was motivated enough to go through all of the math problems in that preparation book three different times. If you decide it is necessary to enroll your child in a course to either prepare or do remedial work, then do it. It is not a reflection of a job poorly done, but a reflection on the examination's poor choice of testing material. If you find your child is unwilling to prepare for examinations then maybe you should rethink whether you'll assist him in going to college. Personally, I like to see effort on the part of the student which proves to me that they really want to go for the right reasons and are willing to work hard.

If a portfolio ultimately takes the place of a transcript and becomes of utmost importance, then create a well-rounded portfolio exposing the diverse and in-depth material your child has "mastered."

You and your child have many options. There are liberal arts colleges that provide a wonderful preparation for many careers and to any graduate work, including the medical field (which is the case with my personal physician). The number of colleges and their specialties is too big of a subject for me to address here, you will have to conduct your own research. I have found the reference area of my library to have books filled with colleges and university's names and locations. Start researching tuition and entrance requirements as early as possible. There is a good chance the knowledge you gain will effect some critical choices including the material covered and the way you record advancement.

Don't forget, after a broad education, there is nothing wrong with entering technical school to be trained in a marketable job or a field that suits the child's talents. Not everybody is college bound and I think we place too much importance on the "degree." In some cases it merely represents that someone had the time and the money to pursue an education that in many instances others did not have. However, it is important to research careers that interest your child and if higher education is necessary, provide the opportunities and resources needed.

We all have weighty decisions ahead of us regarding our children, but let's not shortchange them on an abundant and exciting Charlotte Mason education out of fear of the unknown.

TEN

Coping Strategies

I have met thousands of home schooling parents and I find that many of your concerns zero in on a couple of areas. Quite frequently families seem to need some coping strategies in order to continue to home educate.

Hopefully, these ideas will cover many situations such as, burnout, physical illness resulting in surgery or some convalescing time, or caring for a sick loved one. Whether you suddenly find yourself occupied with something that will keep you from home schooling (so that you will not be able to be actively involved with your children) or you have some advance warning try going back to the three R's.

In a Charlotte Mason education we include so much more than just basic academics that it may not seem "okay" to revert back to workbooks, packets or textbooks in a time of need. Let me reassure you, it is okay. The key to using workbooks as a coping mechanism is to train each child how to maneuver in his book without *any* assistance. This is very important; it may be necessary to choose books that are *a grade level behind* your child's capabilities in order to ensure you will not be needed to interpret the directions. Your child may not advance as quickly as when you work with him on grade level, but he is not going to lose ground which is very important.

Many workbook or packet systems are self contained—the child must master it on his own before moving on. Some parents rely on these systems perpetually, I'm not suggesting that, especially not in a Charlotte Mason book. I'm advising it as a temporary coping strategy only. You'll find that combining the power of habit with some independent materials will result in home school going on without you.

It really helps to stop and rethink your priorities fairly often. I have a rather large family and at times I'll find that one of the children is in special need of my time whether it's because she is slipping behind academically or she simply "needs" my individual attention as a mother. When that happens everyone other than the targeted child can be placed in workbooks, as described above, which gives me the time I need to work intensely with the one child. Again, this would be a temporary situation—the usual goal is to enjoy the full Charlotte Mason method with all of its benefits.

Illness is not the only reason for the need to cope. People with determined personalities, like myself, can become overly reliant on their own abilities. Sheer will power can enable you to continue through home schooling but eventually a crisis can exceed the power of our human determination.

Burnout is definitely a crisis for people who educate children. It is a conflict of huge proportions when those who love children and feel called to work with them grow weary of the task. I have often felt the need to speak plainly about the severity of burnout and the general difficulty of home educating itself. When a parent struggles with any aspect of educating their children the first thing they need is for someone to acknowledge the hardship rather than dismiss it as nonexistent. After the emotions have been acknowledged then solutions can be sought. A Charlotte Mason support group is especially beneficial in these instances. See the question and answer chapter and check the segment on support groups for more detailed information. As I dedicate this chapter to coping I have to first direct our attention to one strategy that may prove to be the most effective.

You may or may not have religious beliefs. If your faith is based on any form of Christianity then I am sure you have noticed the overall lack of agreement on almost every topic. Debates run rampant both between the denominations and within them and they are far to numerous to list here. But, I have found one topic that is never debated. It is acceptable in any denomination to leave our burdens with our Creator. I am going to unashamedly encourage you to try it if you haven't before, resume it, if you've stopped, and keep doing it if you've always done it. I could quote chapter and verse to make my point, but I think the burden bearing attributes of the Lord are well known within each one of us.

There is another condition that can bring on the need for coping. Now and then we all get a case of "bad Mom." This condition can strike without warning. Only a "bad Mom" would complain about her children, or find herself day dreaming of first winning the lottery and then applying her winnings to boarding school. This self condemnation can creep up on us after several days of being behind in laundry, grocery shopping, bathing, etc. It's behind that less than lovely thought, "what if I'm not covering enough math, history, phonics."

Anybody can catch a case of this whether we deserve it or not—and when it occurs during burnout I contend that we do not deserve it. A prerequisite of burnout is that you have to be burning. We who have dedicated our lives to bearing, raising, rearing, training, cleaning, feeding, comforting and yes, educating our young are at the least glowing if not burning.

Bad Mom often starts with comparison, either with another home schooling mother or with the accomplishments of another home schooling student. My advice is to avoid comparisons, and if you can't avoid them then at least be realistic. If you were you able to be the "fly on the wall" in any home schooling household only heaven knows what you'd be likely to see.

The only comparison I recommend is with public school. Call the principal of your local public school and ask permission to sit in for a half or full day as a visitor. To ensure they will allow you to visit act positive and slightly curious. The best pretense to use is, you have been home schooling awhile and you want to see what your student would be experiencing if they were attending this school. Almost any other excuse will go over as well as asking for special permission to deal drugs to the student body for the day. Unless you use this rationale it is unlikely you will be allowed on the campus. Forget your rights as a taxpayer, if they don't want to cooperate you will not have a successful visit.

Pack your bullet proof vest and proceed. Spend as much time as they allow. Mingle with the students and observe the teachers interacting with a classroom. I've done this several times and the outcome is always an overwhelming sense of confidence in my ability to educate my children. I often return from these visits saying, "If I can't do a better job with both hands tied behind my back and drunk then there's something wrong with me."

Another cure for "bad mom" is don't try to be "super mom." When motherhood or home schooling is getting you down stop and simplify. So often when we have a problem we try to attack it with a huge monumental overhaul of the situation. Just like Charlotte Mason's teaching on the formation of good habits, try to implement one habit or idea at a time. Don't write a big list of things you want changed and post it on the living room wall. Success depends on setting one small goal at a time for ourselves and our children and achieving it. It's also a mistake to have "super-make-up-for-a-bad-week" home school day. No one will benefit from this kind of penance. When coping strategies are called for try doing a little tiny bit of school everyday. You will feel better about a little progress made every day when the end of the week comes, than some panicky, hysterical, make-up day.

All in all I find Charlotte Mason to be rather convicting regarding the use of our time, and when we follow her advice and accomplish our goals for the day we'll find we have some free time left. It is absolutely crucial to take time for yourself. This is a serious necessity for home schooling mothers, and we need the support of our families to accomplish it. Don't wait until you're on the brink of collapse to establish the habit of taking time for yourself. Children can be trained to honor your attempts, and your husband must be kept informed of your needs so he can be of help to you.

In Charlotte Mason's era it was common to have domestic help, something present-day housewives, for the most part, do without. If you can afford *any* help at all then I advise you to get it. I think of it as a home school janitorial service. Your family might consider forgoing a luxury such as your weekly delivered pizza and instead substitute two hours a week cleaning assistance.

You need to know when to take a break. If you think you're too busy and don't have any spare time, you need to make some—no excuses. There is a good chance that my life is every bit as busy as yours, and like you, I've had to strike the balance between my duties and my personal sanity. Has your husband ever come to you with that desperate-for-clean-shirts look in his eyes and asked you for suggestions? Instead of pointing out that your next-door neighbor is about his size, it would probably be more appropriate to keep your laundry current or start using a laundry service that includes pressing those shirts. I know you carry a lot of responsibilities and you need to be just that, responsible, but after you've finished meeting everyone else's needs you have a responsibility to look after yourself as well.

Kill two birds with one stone by enjoying some quiet time reading books that restore you and at the same time inspire you with constructive ideas. One suggestion for this is, *Victorian Family Celebrations,* also known as *Mrs. Sharp's Traditions.* Many of you already own this book but I like to remind mothers of it because you'll find encouragement, inspiration and some concrete ideas on how to raise a family and enjoy spending time together. The first part of the book covers topics such as mealtimes, bath and bedtime rituals, family night and how to achieve harmony in the home. The emphasis is placed on how to have an orderly yet happy home. Because home school families spend a lot of time together, I think we can all benefit from fresh ideas.

The remainder of the book covers all the months of the year and gives hundreds of ideas, activities, even recipes appropriate to the seasons and holidays. You do not have to be a follower of birthday or holiday observances to glean some very good ideas of how to enjoy being at home with your children. The author's name is Sarah Ban Breathnach, the ISBN is 0-671-78408-0. Also check your library for availability.

There are many books that mom's find refreshing. For many it's the Bible, poetry, fiction or even a magazine. We home schooling parents read so much research type of writing and have to spend time in the education catalogs that sometimes we have to make ourselves stop and read something for the simple pleasure of reading. I have found the answer for me is poetry. The reason it's refreshing is you put in as much effort as you want. When all your reading has been for studying then it feels good to read words that simply have beauty and rhythm. You *can* work your brain if you want when reading poetry or you can just relax and enjoy it.

Another valid coping solution is to cooperate with other home schooling families. Many of the support groups have expanded to the point where they can offer very sophisticated co-ops. Various classes are offered either utilizing the parents or by bringing in experts such as artists or mechanics. Ordinarily, participation on the part of the parent is optional—of course if too many parents want a day off and don't want to take a turn teaching then the concept fails. My concerns would include that the co-op itself is run by home schooling parents who completely understand the situation and that they would be offered free of charge. Many of us do not have the extra money so often required for groups like this. Why not start a Charlotte Mason co-op? It may be just what the doctor ordered if you're nearing burnout. Even if you're coping very well at this point it would be nice if you could alleviate someone else's distress.

Not all public school districts are the same. Schools and individual teachers vary greatly. The first home schooling parents in the United States were not able to access the public school on a part-time basis. Things have greatly changed for the better and some schools have determined to be of help to home schooled children by offering new options including part-time enrollment. Ordinarily, it works this way. The child is enrolled as a home schooled student but he can access up to three classes a day. Typically, the class choices are band, foreign language, math or science. Academics and electives are both available. These improvements on the part of the school are changing the face of home schooling. Some veteran home schooling parents look back on the "us and them" days and have problems accepting these changes. Newer home educators didn't have to fight for the legal right to home school and tend to partake of these opportunities without reservation. I'm broaching the subject under the topic of coping because I want to invite you to think for yourself. Home schooling parents fall into peer pressure as easily as any other group. Some seem to make decisions for their child's education as though they're involved in a popularity contest—afraid to cross philosophical ideals with their friends. Each child is entitled to the individual treatment that best suits his needs. There is no one correct method to home educate, and there is no one formula to follow. Perhaps the best coping mechanism for some is to combine home education with public education to receive the best of both worlds.

It's okay to need a break from your own children. Maybe you just tripped over your son's size 13 foot for the tenth time today just as he was asking you how to spell "America." Every now and then we are going to look around and ask ourselves "Why?" Sometimes, (especially when we get into our second decade of home school) it occurs to the mother that her children never leave. They are always around, underfoot (or on your foot). I've met a mom (or two) who held to very strict convictions that a good mother never needs a break. I can't agree with that. I know I need time away from my little darlings and it makes me a better parent to get that break. So in case you were waiting for someone to do it, I'll give you permission to (temporarily) retreat from the responsibilities of home management and home schooling. Charlotte also mentioned the subject of spending too much time with the children.

I'm currently on the other side of the "Isolation is next to Godliness" teaching. Some isolation is very effective for making certain that some education is occurring but overdoing the isolation is one of several home school trends I've observed. Others may have benefited from the teaching that "godly women rarely leave home." I'm happy I broke free from this teaching and I'm glad to be out living my life. I think my children may have suffered from too much isolation as well. If you've been under "a good mom does not need breaks" or "a good mom does not seek the help of others" or if your children are becoming "ingrown," by that I mean turned into themselves, take a new look at your life. Chances are, suffering in silence will only work temporally with possible burnout surfacing when you least expect and with possibly dire consequences.

Another coping strategy is to get organized. Regardless of where you physically conduct your home school, some basic tidiness can soothe rattled nerves. Having boxes assigned to each child has helped me tremendously. I like to buy those that stack and have ample room. If you buy them all at the same time it's easier to make sure they're compatible. Knowing where your materials are saves time and keeps your stress level down. Nothing is worse than spending any amount of time looking under beds and in dog houses for missing math books.

Menu planning can save valuable time. And what, my friend, is more valuable to the home schooling mother than time? I sit down with my children when we are all very, very, hungry and we brainstorm about breakfast, lunch and dinner. We make a huge list of meals we like. The more you think of the better. The list can be kept in a computer file and added to from time to time. Years ago, I also made a master grocery list, and the funny thing is, people always wanted a copy. The best way to make one is to think of how your grocery store is laid out and group your regular purchases accordingly. Most trips I make to the store start with me hitting "print" for the list and using a yellow highlighter to mark what I need. I don't do this so I can look like a show-off at the store, it really helps me. Many families benefit from freezer cooking and it has become very well known. I recommend the book *Frozen Assets, How to Cook for a Day and Eat for a Month*, by Deborah Taylor-Hough.

Learning how to occupy preschoolers during the school hours can help you to cope better during school. Even preschoolers are subject to habits. They can be trained over time to play quietly while everyone else studies. It will take work on your part to teach them that it is not okay to walk around finding ways to be mischievous and disruptive. The same thing applies to your youngest students who finish earlier than older students. Let me emphasize the work involved with this task. This is by far one the most often asked questions by all home schoolers because it is not easy to deal with. There aren't any easy answers either and we need to acknowledge the difficulty of the situation. Last time I visited the local school classroom the teacher did not have an unruly preschooler running wildly through the room and a baby to nurse.

So what can we do other than accept this difficulty with as much grace as possible? Try having a school box exactly like the other children with your preschooler's name on it. Stock it with safety scissors, crayons, color books, lacing cards, quiet toys and all of that kind of stuff. Sometimes the young child will want to be like your older kids and look occupied with something important and sometimes they'll want to run around and play. They don't have the self control, usually, to sit for any length of time—that's why they're not in school yet. Preschoolers often want to work in the same book as the older sister. That problem is easily solved by giving young children used up workbooks. None of my little kids have cared that they were already written in, it's the appearance of looking like they are important enough to "do" school like the big kids that matters.

If you find a particular child comes into your life that is so distracting that nobody can get anything done around them, then perhaps you need to remove the child from the school area. Waiting until her nap time is one solution that worked for me. We couldn't get the whole school day accomplished in that short time but we could save the most important subjects for then. Plus, I don't see anything wrong with the child watching educational videos for thirty minutes to an hour while the rest of the children get a chance to concentrate.

You could sit and play with clay or whatever your preschooler likes to do but watch out for manipulation. She sees you paying attention to the other children and her goal may be to hog you to herself. Be strong and be the adult. The education of your other children is important and the good news is that the preschooler will mature and soon take her place with the others.

As mentioned in the planning chapter, I've had all of us (myself included) wear the same colored T-shirt which signifies it's school time. This visual aid helps the immature mind in the training of habits. When the shirts are replaced by regular clothes (they're usually worn over our clothes) then school is over for the day.

Some people cope with the home schooling blues by going shopping for some educational "pick-me-up" such as some new books or games. This can be invigorating but don't make the mistake of trying to find contentment through unnecessary spending—quite often it's ineffective.

There might be better things than shopping to calm yourself with. Some possibilities I can think of include prayer, listening to music, playing an instrument, exercise, service projects, visiting friends or relatives, painting and sewing. In other words, think back to before you had children if necessary and recall the pastimes and interests and talents you once had time to enjoy.

Maybe it has been too long since you played. As we know, all work and no play makes mom a dull girl. Perhaps the best coping strategy you'll ever find is being outdoors. We know Charlotte Mason would approve of that!

ODE TO ALL COMMITTED *(or soon to be)* HOME SCHOOLERS EVERYWHERE
by amateur poet, Catherine Levison

The ant farm just spilled all over the floor,
Last year's science project's walking out the front door,
The in-laws left a message, they want to stay awhile,
And your church has discovered they have a pedophile.

You're chronically late to home school P. E.
The phone always rings when you're about to leave.
Your coat's always covered in cat hair,
Once again the husband's out of clean underwear.

Your friend needs help, her twins have the flu,
The kids are holding the plunger asking *you* what to do,
Your inquiries about the toilet are answered with "I don't know."
In the distance you hear "Hey, where's my Play-doh™?"

It's time to make lunch but there's nothing to eat.
The postcard in your hand says they've canceled your retreat,
Your stress level hits an all time high,
You can *see* the kids on the bus waving good-bye.

The play is tonight but your kids haven't rehearsed,
But just when things can't get any worse,
The town gossip assures you "your secret's safe with me,
I've only told two people, or maybe it was three."

Stolen moments in the shower (worrying about grocery money),
You hear "MOM, MOM, the baby looks *funny*,"
A brief struggle later (of course you're dripping wet),
Hallelujah, you've retrieved the barrette.

Turns out the Latin phrase you've posted has a dirty connotation,
And your husband has determined to work through his vacation,
The math books you've been waiting for are late in arriving,
The lap top you found floating has no chance for surviving.

The kids come in from playing pronouncing their new "word"
Of course it's of the variety you wish they never heard,
Just then you find your three year old is covered in bumps,
That's okay, at least you're all over the mumps.

Phone rings again "You know the meeting's at *your* house!"
But your caller in competing with "Ed just knocked my tooth out."
Your five year old is threatening to run away,
You owe some allowance and he wants you to pay.

Here comes your neurotic neighbor again,
the one that always reeks of gin (?),
She's not sure if you want to know,
Your son was squirting Mrs. Jones a minute ago.

Another day's over, you've used your time well,
It's time to take off your jean apparel,
Jump in those jammies, let your cares float away,
If anyone wakes you there will be "heck" to pay.

When quitting altogether is a temptation to you,
You've got a case of "WHY am I home schooling blues?!"
Don't pack your bags and run away,
Turn toward heaven and pray, pray, pray.

ELEVEN

Book Selection

*M*any people come to a point in their Charlotte Mason understanding where they realize that most of her methods are actually working for them. They've learned, applied and conquered the primary techniques of art appreciation, narration and they could define a whole book with the best of them.

They've started collecting books, and everything seems to be going well when universally they run into a couple of problems. One of which is "I can't find the books Charlotte recommended." or "I can't find the books that fit my plan."

Let's take the subject of history because when one first begins to find living books they tend to actually start a collection of American history books without intending to do so. Why? Because of the abundance of living books on United States history—they are far easier to locate than living books on Europe, Canada, South America or Australia. Considering the brief time period of United States history (even including discovery, colonization and the revolt), there sure are a lot of books available on this relatively young country.

One immediate solution in the area of history might be to read biographies of missionaries (a particularly helpful idea for the more obscure countries). In addition, developing a pen pal relationship either through the missionary outreach of your church or from the internet can result in a recommended reading list of great books about that country. Doing this myself has resulted in the ability to cover European history using living books. Many of my favorite books were shipped to me from my English pen pal. She was able to locate many of the books from my wish list. When I corresponded with folks in Australia I asked about their history and the books that would best describe their country.

Your need to find appropriate books can possibly be solved by using book lists. We have a great many of these lists available to us—some are geared to the Charlotte Mason parent and some are not. One often recommend book list is *Let the Authors Speak* by Carolyn Hatcher, and I've heard good things about *Books Children Love* by Elizabeth Wilson. Both are easily obtained through most home school catalogs. Currently, people are very excited about *All Through the Ages*, by Christine Miller. She, too, has labored long and hard to provide a well organized list of history books of a literary quality. Her address is 1015-M S. Taft Hill Rd. #263, Ft. Collins, CO 80521. There are lists available on the Charlotte Mason web sites too. I've added a book list in the appendix that I hope you'll find helpful.

A similar solution would be the educational or home school supply catalogs. Many of the catalogs serve as a recommended reading list and you know right where you can get the book. I recommend finding one or two of these that *you* can really trust. One of my personal favorites is Lifetime Books and Gifts. They carry one the largest *quality* inventories in the United States and the owners are home educators. You can call them for a catalog at 800-377-0390. Once you become familiar with the convictions, motives and literary taste of any given catalog you may be able to order sight unseen with relative confidence.

Some of my classic book sets I collect have lists of all the other books they publish in that set. I've found those to be great suggested reading lists. If you don't already own a set look at book stores and libraries.

Obviously, book lists and catalogs will not always solve the problem of how to find books to match the topic you want to cover. While it can be satisfying to choose a topic and then go looking for interesting books that will sufficiently cover it—you may find it can be far more difficult and more time consuming than you had planned. All of us have had this disappointment, perhaps most commonly at the library when it becomes apparent that everyone else in town is studying our topic. Another great place to conduct research in the internet—Amazon.Com, for one, will "hunt" for out-of-print books for you.

It comes down to this. Should you decide on a topic and then go looking for the right books? Or, can you eliminate this obstacle by becoming so skilled at book collecting that you have a great assortment of quality books at your fingertips? To accomplish this, you'll have to let go of any borderline neurotic impulses to cover everything you think the public school is covering (but really isn't). You'll have to adopt Charlotte Mason's philosophy that "the best thought the world possesses is stored in books; we must open books to children, the best books; our own concern is abundant provision and orderly serving." (Vol. 6, p. 26)

That brings up the most important point—there is a skill to be learned. You need to learn to ascertain the value of a book at every opportunity, at a moment's notice. That is the key to a great collection. In other words, it could be considered your *job* to locate interesting books, and, because it's a little like searching for a needle in a haystack, you have to always be looking. Think of yourself as a hunter, your eyes always aware of your surroundings. Every trip to the thrift store, garage sale or your Aunt Hilda's attic may result in the find of a lifetime. With effort your collection will grow. Simultaneously, you should begin to eliminate the worthless books from your shelves, thus making room for your living and whole books.

Can you overdo it? Yes and no. If you find your long-lost talent is book collecting and take to it with a zeal (or obsession) that makes for family trouble such as "sneaking" books in behind your husband's back, raiding the savings account (again!) or going without meals, then, yes, you are overdoing it. But for most of us I don't know that we could ever have too many beautifully written books on a wide variety of subjects. This is our goal according to Charlotte, "We owe it to every child to put him in communication with the great minds that he may get at the great thoughts; with the minds, that is, of those who have left us great works; and the only vital method of education appears to be that children should read worthy books, many worthy books."

Not every attempt to locate a living book will be successful. I have left many stores without a book under my arm. Congratulate yourself when this happens, it indicates that you have become more selective. When I finally locate a living book that I can't live without, I buy it *whether I was planning to cover that topic or not.* Possibly, one of my high school students will read it independently and even if I don't get around to using it during school it is still worthy enough to sit on my shelf and wait, if necessary, for the following generation.

While a book is waiting for use, it decorates my home. Older, antique, books have a beauty all their own that hardly needs embellishing. I collect book ends and doilies so any flat surface becomes a book shelf. Newer books also have a great look. It isn't often that a book that is so ugly it needs to be tucked away out of sight. There are books covering the topic of how to store book collections such as, *At Home with Books: How Booklovers Live and Care for Their Libraries*, by Estelle Ellis and Caroline Seebohm ISBN 0-517-59500-1. Also available is, *A Passion for Books*, by Terry Glaspey ISBN 1-56507-781-4. Decorating with books also helps with the "out of sight, out of mind problem" I've had with home schooling products I've purchased. When you see it, dust it and generally live with it everyday, it's easier to remember to use it in school.

The end result of a good collection is that you can plan a study of a person, century, country or ocean based on the books you own. In fact having great books around can inspire you to cover topics that you might not have otherwise considered. Please don't misunderstand, I am not suggesting you become a slave to your collection. On the contrary, you would always be free to cover something like European history without owning a single book on it.

When collecting books one idea to keep in mind is Charlotte's suggestion that we cover one man or one country for a long amount of time with a *substantial* book rather than the textbook style of covering massive amounts of history in short snippets. I agree with her that to know something well and retain at least some information on it, it's better to really dive in, pay attention and spend serious time on it. The outcome of studying one man for one year would be: An awareness of the country he lived in, what the people around him were like, what the political structure was, or whether they lived well or suffered under tyranny, plagues, economical devastation, chronic wars or a caste system. I believe spending substantial time results in retained knowledge. Without a doubt one of the best explanations of Charlotte Mason's philosophy of books was written by J. P. Inman who stated it this way. "She was a great believer in Big Books. Great literature speaks for itself and an author is his own best expounder. The poet and the writer can speak directly to the soul of the child. What cannot be understood directly can well wait for another time. A great author writes not that he may be expounded, but that he may ring a bell in the secret chambers of the heart." (*Charlotte Mason College,* p. 8)

Textbooks

Charlotte Mason families usually follow the concept of using a whole book that covers one topic. However at times it's advantageous to use a normal textbook or a living textbook. Either can be used as it is designed or used as a backbone where you could fill in with living/whole books. For example, if the science textbook covers electricity we could read that portion and then locate a whole book on Thomas Edison or Benjamin Franklin. After conducting some experiments (careful with those electrical ones) and possibly visiting the science museum or some other field trip, we could return to the textbook to see what else we might cover. This format provides structure, and sometimes comfort, to those who do not want to write their own curriculum. A word to the wise on textbooks—they may not even cover some topics that you consider to be a priority. On the other hand, if the book is comprehensive then the basic downfall is in the attempt to get around to everything, they ordinarily have to rely on summarizing, resulting in a lack of detail.

Living Textbooks

There are many books that would fall under the category of a living textbook and some of them are truly great finds. There are several definitions as well. One might be the kind of book that is close to being a living book because of its biographical information but is still "snippet-y." For instance, *Spiritual Lives of the Great Composers* and *Mathematicians are People Too* (and their sequels) are books I own and use. While I recommend both of them, they are *not substantial books covering an entire life* by including ample details. Both books have *brief* biographies and quickly move on to the next life. One drawback they hold in common is when read cover to cover (or even partially), they yield very little retention. Too many people are covered too rapidly, and confusion of details is the end result. Powerful memory or not, when one tries to recall which composer had a large family and which one died childless you will find it difficult to remember. The solution might be to choose one historical figure, starting with either of these books and spend a month or two following up on the material covered.

Another attribute that sets a living textbook apart from a normal textbook is its use of literary language. Anytime we choose a book we want to look for that quality.

Lastly, the living textbook is written in a narrative style. This brings up the important point that a valuable book can be overlooked and discarded due to its textbook look. As we do not judge a book by its cover, we should not judge a book by its format. Don't miss out on a great book just because it has paragraph titles. Narrative textbooks are available in used bookstores, and there are good ones still in print.

In conclusion, let me say that many parents are asking for a Charlotte Mason scope and sequence or curriculum. While this is not a wrong desire we need to understand the limitations one individual's curriculum would have. Literary taste varies from person to person— likewise convictions and the resulting discrimination. A book one person might deem worthy is in another's discard pile. A book I might treasure as my all-time favorite you may consider to be the world's worst book. A case in point would be if a reviewer has ever let you down (and odds are they will eventually), then you're familiar with the disappointment that results from finally having a recommended book arrive only to find out it isn't at all what you expected it to be. Even more important is if the reviewer (or curriculum writer) has a motive (e.g., selling the products they recommend), then you have to weigh their advice even more.

Some people are looking to England as the only plausible source of a future curriculum. This too could result in disappointment. I think we only need to look at Bobby Scott's interview (granted for the discontinued *Charlotte Mason Communiqué*) to recognize that if those currently involved in the PNEU aren't even reading the Charlotte Mason books, then how can we expect them to write an adequate curriculum or book list.

Aside from who writes the list, it will only be as valuable as the books are *available*. If you can't obtain the recommended book, it isn't going to be helpful to you. A great percentage of my C. Mason finds are not generally available. No one enjoys conducting a thorough search (like the two-year-long one I just conducted) with the end result of not obtaining or even having temporary access to one of the books Charlotte

Mason wrote about. I can't even look at it to see what she liked about it. I don't want to create false hopes (when I write) about a book that you ultimately won't be able to find. And I don't want false despair that would make you believe you cannot do the Charlotte Mason method without certain books in your possession.

We have to also be careful not to limit ourselves to only books that were directly named by Charlotte herself, not only because many are inaccessible today, but we also need to recognize there have been thousands of valuable books written since her death. I believe she would be the first to tell us we had made a foolish decision and taken her preferences too literally.

This method seems to attract book lovers and Charlotte was one herself. She spent time looking for great, affordable works for her students. We can look at lists (like the one provided in the appendix), make and take recommendations, but ultimately we have to locate them ourselves. It seems to be a good use of a book lover's time.

TWELVE

Charlotte Mason in the Classroom

Charlotte Mason's method has been used in countless classrooms for the last hundred years and it continues to be used across the world. Currently there are twenty PNEU schools in England still using her method and the United States has at least twenty Charlotte Mason based schools.

Home schooling parents may at some point find themselves with an opportunity to teach in a classroom setting. Some examples would include teaching at a home school co-op, helping at a school or leading a Sunday school class. You may have acquaintances, neighbors or relatives who teach in classrooms or perhaps one of your children will choose a teaching career.

Ordinarily my objective is to weed through mountains of available information on how Charlotte Mason's methods were used in the classroom and then make the translation to home schooling. Reading about this topic is helpful, however, observation is even more beneficial. I have been able to visit a few schools using Mason's techniques and I've interviewed several teachers from all over the country who are involved with the method in a classroom setting. An American school principal of a Charlotte Mason based school also granted me an interview which I found most helpful. He had made frequent trips to England to observe the current PNEU schools. He found that they keep many of the techniques in use with the exception of narration.

In my opinion narration should not be abandoned in the classroom. I believe narration will prove to be one of the most helpful tools. I made use of it when I volunteered as a tour guide. People quickly caught on that I expected them to be able to repeat what they had learned. They seemed to enjoy being called on and it kept them alert to *everything* I said.

Jenny King, Elsie Kitching, G. F. Husband, E. K. Manders, Essex Cholmondeley and Helen Wix have all written about narration in the classroom. There are significant differences between its use in the home school and its use with classrooms.

Prior preparation by the teacher is recommended. First read the passage so that you are familiar with it. Watch for unusual words that your students (whether children or adults) will not know. These need to be defined before the reading takes place. If a white board is available have the words, with a brief definition, displayed during the reading and the narration.

Further preparation includes reading the passage and thinking through the material. Put it aside and give your mind time to process the story and narrate it to yourself mentally. This will help you to practice masterly inactivity later when the class listens and narrates the passage. It will enable you to let the student's mind act on the material and prepare you to stand aside as much as possible. Reflect on the main point of the reading until you clearly know the focus or the primary teaching of the material. This too will prepare you to help the students in an inconspicuous manner. Religious topics, for example, often need more contemplation time than academic subjects in order to grasp the spiritual meaning.

Think of connecting questions from the last session (whether it occurred the week before or the day before) that will help the students to remember your last meeting. This is different from questioning directly following the reading—that is to be avoided. G. F. Husband defended the use of narration over the practice of questioning quite well when he pointed out that the real thinking was done by the one who designed the question. When one relies on narration you'll find the student will supply both the question and the answer. If you'd like to avoid questioning try presenting a brief summary yourself or asking a class member to do so. The goal is to remind everyone, even yourself, of what you covered last time. You'll find the students often remember better than the teacher what was previously learned.

Determine whether you'll need any visual aids. Quite often the PNEU position was that visuals are rather unnecessary and sometimes distracting. Those involved in Sunday school teaching agreed as well. However, a well-chosen map or piece of artwork will embellish the teaching while bringing some life to the lesson, especially when used infrequently and not overly relied upon.

In classrooms we want to begin each lesson by introducing the names, dates, pictures and difficult words. Follow with reading the passage, remembering to regulate the length of the reading. Limit yourself to ten to fifteen minutes at a time. Hopefully, your well-chosen passage will hold the attention of the group because of its literary quality and the fact that it is exceedingly interesting. The way you read will also make a huge difference. You are not going to reread the passage so you must be clear and articulate. Try reading as though it was the most interesting thing you've ever read—it's good to apply yourself but don't be overly dramatic or phony. If you're using a book that everyone can bring with them such as a Bible then allow them to follow along with you as you read.

Narration has to occur immediately following the reading. No one knows ahead of time who will do the narrating so everyone has to apply themselves to listening. Ask for volunteers or call on someone and allow them a few comments. In classrooms we have more than one child narrate (unlike home school) but we do not have one child start at the beginning, give his narration to completion and then call on another to start at the beginning. Instead think of it as popcorn with kernels popping all over the room one at time as you call on them. Kindly interrupt one child for the purpose of calling on another. This is especially helpful when the narrator has made an error. Rather than correcting it yourself, stop the student and call upon someone else, they will usually get it right and make the correction for you. In general, keep in mind that children remember best and think more when they discover things for themselves. Your part is to listen enthusiastically. Let the narrators bring out the key points. If you're carefully applying masterly inactivity you'll find ways to draw from the class any necessary corrections, emphasis or important facts through discussion and very minimal questioning.

Do not expect to hear extraordinary narrations every time. In some classroom situations students come irregularly and they may be unaccustomed to narrating or have a shy personality. Never force a shy child to narrate! Eventually a shy person will make an attempt—praise any effort she makes and don't ask her to continue past the point of what she wants to offer. In small classrooms each child will get a chance to narrate if she wants to participate. There is a big difference between underachievers and shy people. Be as intuitive as possible—good teachers know human nature and use it to everyone's advantage. People caught not listening have to suffer the embarrassment before the group and that itself is the best consequence. Again, you must avoid embarrassing shy people at all costs.

"One chance" reading should be the policy—it is the best way to develop the power of attention. Reviewing and rereading hinder the mind from working at full capacity. Having said that, *some* of the PNEU teachers thought that on rare occasions, *if* there had been a lot of discussion following the narration, then a little rereading of the passage would be in order at the close of the lesson.

The benefits of using narration in a classroom have been noted and written about by many. One of the greatest benefits is how much *more* material can be covered quickly and efficiently. Narration drastically eliminates time wasting techniques such as the pop quiz, the weekly review and the seemingly endless summary questions. Helen Wix wrote in 1917 that children using standard educational techniques were losing interest and not paying attention. She also noted that the teachers worked extremely hard, but they complained about having to teach the same things over and over without the desired results. Time is too valuable to waste—teachers need to find ways to help students to progress.

Narration brings a dynamic to the classroom that provides a chance for everybody to become involved through a shared experience. It gives regular opportunities for students to learn how to express themselves instead of the rare occasion offered by the "oral report." The sheer drain of constant review becomes unnecessary and undesirable; however, the teacher always knows whether the students are grasping what she is trying to communicate.

Written narrations help tremendously with language arts skills. In addition, the more experience the students have with writing the more confidence they'll gain. King reminded us that science and math can be approached the same way. She wrote, "A mind trained by this method brings powers of concentration and accuracy of thought to bear on any matter to be studied."

King also contemplated the use of short lessons in public school classrooms and concluded that in some circumstances the teacher will not be able to use them. When a school district demands that certain subjects be taught for a certain length of time then the only option is to comply. Weekly meetings often have one purpose and one subject eliminating the option of switching subjects. You can use the *idea* of short lessons when you structure the time you have available. Instead of presenting a single topic for the entire time, try offering multiple topics in short segments that relate to the main theme.

In school classrooms you could take Jenny King's advice. She wrote, "The most demanding work in any subject can be done in the morning. Some physical activity should be included every day with some time spent out of doors." I know of a public school in my city that teaches the academics in the morning and spends the afternoons on the fine arts, expressive arts and field trips just as Charlotte Mason would have recommended.

King also wrote that variety, especially with younger children, was of utmost concern. This is achieved by trying for an element of surprise in every lesson. She advocated group work including the use of dramatic representation. You can act out nearly any story, but remember that some children would rather be in the audience than be one of the actors. I would be sensitive to this whenever possible. One way the PNEU schools in England are continuing to practice this is by producing Shakespearean plays on a regular basis.

Like everyone else, King recommended small classrooms as the best environment—however, we know this is not always possible. I was very impressed with her suggestion to this problem. Bring in volunteers from the community. They can listen to individual narrations, read aloud and help tutor children one on one. I know of busy home schooling parents who give of their time in this way and I believe everyone benefits. It would be an excellent opportunity to introduce some of Charlotte's ideals to the public school.

Sunday School

Charlotte Mason's love for children probably served her well as she taught a Sunday school class for twenty–seven years. No doubt she used narration and attempted to make it as interesting as possible. I'm positive that no matter what type of religion you adhere to, you would want excited children and adults in your classes.

Both Charlotte Mason and I hold to Christian beliefs, however if you are of another faith please adapt the following information in any way that suits the situation. If you are not personally involved with Sunday school teaching perhaps you'd like to take a few ideas and share them with the teacher at your church. Ultimately each religious organization and each teacher has the prerogative to choose "what" to teach and "how" to teach. My goal is to provide some ideas used by Charlotte Mason's associates.

The first tip will not surprise you if you're familiar with Mason's teachings. Do not underestimate children. She wrote that lessons designed to "amuse while they instruct" assume the children have weak brains. Instead we want to practice masterly inactively—that means we're going to present challenging material and let them process it with very little interference. Helen Wix noted the only difficulty with this advice is the sheer simplicity of it. She admitted that it can be foreign to teachers to do so little and leave so much to the student.

If the students are adults or children that are old enough to write independently, they could write all their narrations in one special book. Younger children could dictate narrations to the teacher who could record them for the student. They, too, could be kept in one book. This would be very time consuming as you can imagine—perhaps volunteers could be called upon to help. Keep in mind some passages will be harder to narrate than others. When you're covering difficult material and the narrator appears stumped ask him to identify the main theme.

In either the same book or a different one, have the students sketch objects from nature. You could provide small sketchbooks for each student and write their name on the front cover. I suggest that you store them in the classroom and not send them home until the end of the year. Calling this a nature notebook may not go over well in some churches. It may be better to call it *God's Book of Creation* or whatever would be appropriate for the circumstances. When possible take the class outside to sketch. If that is an unlikely event gather specimens to bring to class. Sand dollars are an excellent example of God's creation. They appear to have flowers drawn on them. Ask the class how the design got there, provide some sketch pencils and you'll have some excited students. I predict your parents will also be happy with a little less glitter on the back seat of their cars. This type of "craft" is real. The churches who use sketching in the place of busy work are very satisfied with the results. If you'd rather start small pass out individual sheets of sketch paper rather than books and have the children take those home. If that meets with everyone's approval then you could proceed with individual books.

Don't forget variety. Colorful specimens make for colorful sketchbooks. You'll need to provide colored pencils and perhaps watercolors. This could get expensive. Consider a fundraiser or seeking parent support.

Any book or story read to the class can be illustrated in the sketchbooks. This encourages active listening and provides constructive participation.

Christian poetry could be written in the sketchbook along with hymns pertaining to nature and creation. There are also many Bible verses that would be great additions. Encourage the students to use their best handwriting.

Timelines and/or the book of centuries could be used in a Sunday school setting. It would probably be sufficient to have one for the entire class. At the end of a teaching students could take turns making entries on the appropriate page. This brings up the point that home schooling parents have many resources and ideas at their disposal that could be brought into a Sunday school.

One Charlotte Mason Sunday school teacher I interviewed found visitors needed a little more prompting than the regulars did, but she didn't alter her techniques when new children came. She would read large sections of scripture and prompt with "How did the story start?"

She remembered to challenge their minds by giving them the actual Bible and she avoided the watered down books. She thought it was important to teach them hymns that would stay with them their whole lives rather than silly songs. She managed to forego all curriculum and all busy work. Instead she provided dress up clothes and they acted out the stories they read.

Another Sunday school teacher I know used narration instead of the curriculum. He viewed it as "twaddle" and laid it aside. He kept students interested by letting them use a tape recorder for their narrations. They loved hearing their own voices. He also used his own imagination in other ways and made things as lively as possible—he frequently brought in live animals which truly impressed his class.

Reading Material

Ordinarily when we read aloud Charlotte's way we restrict ourselves to short fifteen to twenty minute segments. This helps to keep the attention of those listening and it makes the material easier to narrate. The natural question is how will you occupy your class for an hour and a half with fifteen minute readings? One answer is to use more than one book. After reading a Bible account (followed by narration) try reading a missionary's or a martyr's account. Any Christian biography would serve the purpose if it met with the Church's approval and was interesting to read. *Pilgrim's Progress* would be a good example of another book that is not watered down. Poetry could also be used. The main goal (according to the PNEU teachers) is to present a new idea about God. Accuracy is important—Rev. Seely taught us not to assume the teaching doesn't matter as long as the students are kept good and amused.

Bible

Charlotte thought that children enjoyed the Bible and she advised that children between the ages of six and nine have a lot of the Bible read to them. Using the actual Bible allows the teaching to reach the child without commentary. She also thought this age group could be memorizing Bible passages. "It is a delightful thing to have the memory stored with beautiful, comforting, and inspiring passages, and we cannot tell when and how this manner of seed may spring up, grow, and bear fruit; but the learning of the parable of the Prodigal Son, for example, should not be laid on the children as a burden. The whole parable should be read to them in a way to bring out its beauty and tenderness;" (Vol. 1 p. 253)

Charlotte was not an advocate of paraphrased versions of the Bible. If you choose to use one, attempt to find the most accurate available. Children are impressionable and they are likely to grow up with mistaken notions of what the Bible said. My favorite example is this. At least half of North America believes that Adam and Eve ate an apple. It wasn't an apple tree. It was the tree of the knowledge of good and evil.

There are other errors frequently taught in the Sunday school room and we should not assume that they will go away as the student matures. Some adults think they know the Bible thoroughly when in reality their knowledge consists of a few stories read to them that may or may not have been true to the original version. Rev. Seeley warned us in Charlotte's magazine not to resort to a *desperate effort to simplify* the Bible risking future disbelief or unbelief. It causes too much confusion and is not our goal when it comes to spiritual truths. Rev. Seeley had seen this at its worst, in fact he claimed he'd witnessed interference with "the necessity of the new birth and of the great work of the Lord Jesus," which of course are two primary aspects of the gospel itself.

Even very young children need to have the actual scripture read to them without making it weary. We have to be very careful not to make it a burden or cause a dislike for the Bible.

Rev. Seeley warned us to not inadvertently teach that if children "try to do their best, and avoid disobedience, falsehood, and other gross faults, God will be so pleased with them that He will take them to heaven when they die." This is the opposite of the gospel. If that was the ticket to heaven we would not need a savior, we could have done it without Him.

The PNEU Sunday School teachers also noted that the parent or teacher needs to become familiar with the Bible in order to successfully instruct young people. Wisdom comes from reading the Bible itself referring to parallel passages, asking the Holy Spirit for help. It's also helpful to use scriptural terms when teaching Biblical doctrines. You can only do that if you, yourself, know them.

One of them also noted that the more the Sunday school teacher knows of the Bible the better. When a teacher speaks of the Bible his love for it should show. You will know you've done your duty when the children are reading it themselves privately for their own pleasure and for their own instruction.

Knowledge of the Bible as a whole will make good theologians of your students. Let's help them to know its general scope and how to handle it. That way children will learn their doctrines themselves and know how to avoid false doctrine and how to reply to false teaching. This is the best way to prepare them for adulthood.

Art in Sunday School

Charlotte and her associates warned against using visual aids to excess in the Sunday school room. However, carefully chosen masterpiece art that is truly magnificent is a welcome enhancement. According to Seeley we want to avoid misleading symbols in the art. He noted the mother Mary has been depicted in many unrealistic settings. Often she appears dressed as a nun seated among various religious symbols. If we try to locate art that is the nearest to the truth, we would want to keep in mind that Mary was Jewish and she probably lived more the peasant's lifestyle than she is sometimes portrayed. Seeley recommended we tell our students that the artist made his own interpretation, if necessary.

Something I view as valuable is how much art has been inspired by the Bible. Many art books are dedicated to the theme and we have enjoyed several of them. When the Venetian exhibit came to the Seattle Art Museum it contained about seventy percent Biblical art. That is quite a testimony to children. We want them to see how the Bible has inspired some of the greatest artists that our world has ever known and how they chose to express their thoughts into beautiful masterpieces.

THIRTEEN

Questions & Answers

$\mathscr{I}$have been asked almost every conceivable question about Charlotte Mason and her method that you could ever imagine. Some of them I can answer, some can only be speculated on and some I just don't know how to answer. This section represents a few of the commonly asked questions.

Do the children really have to sit still when they're being read to? I have a kinetic learner.

There is much attention placed on learning styles in home education and I do have a high regard for the basic philosophy. However, when I attended a seminar on the topic I learned something new. The teacher gave all of us a test to determine our learning style. I knew the common options were, visual, auditory and kinetic and I strongly believed my test would confirm a strong tendency to be a visual learner. When my results showed that I was a little of everything my reaction was, "Oh great, now I find out I have some problem I didn't know I had."

Fortunately for me, everyone in the room had the same results. When I inquired about these unpredictable results the teacher told us that a mixture is normal, almost all people will exhibit all three styles and in fact, it is the goal.

We do know that some children can lean heavily toward one of the styles and I am often asked how to cope with kinetic and visual learners when we want to read aloud to our children and have them narrate what they have comprehended.

I look at it this way. Technically, everybody has to learn how to listen. Some people excel at it and some don't. When your child reaches adulthood he will make a better impression on his customers, bosses, peer group and spouse if he can listen well and make his body (including his face) look as if he were listening.

Imagine sitting in your doctor's office wearing your "gown" while perched at the end of the examination table. You are trying to explain your symptoms to a doctor who is juggling pencils with a distracted look on his face. He assures you he's listening, he just needs to move when he's thinking. Picture a board room full of executives and dignitaries waiting for the annual report to be presented by a young man running in circles around the meeting table. Think back to the last time you had a crisis in your life and you desperately needed to talk it over with a friend. Who did you call? Your self-absorbed friend who has a diagnosable listening deficit or your friend who has trained herself to hear what you're saying, and remember it long enough to make meaningful comments on what you shared. Husbands are another group that either have it or they don't. I think all wives would appreciate a listening husband. Charlotte Mason wrote, "There are more people who can talk than who can listen . . . to listen with all one's mind is an act of delicate courtesy which draws the best out of even dull people."

My point is, even if a child has a strength in an area other than listening it will do him good to concentrate on listening skills. Being a good listener is very important to professions such as lawyers, doctors, accountants—it is equally important for contractors, plumbers and mechanics.

Parents will sometimes come to the child's defense by telling me that the child is listening adequately despite his activity. They claim Junior can tell them what has been taught. My answer is everyone wants to *feel* listened to and that is accomplished through "body language." Active people can improve in this area through short practice sessions.

How do you make the transition from other methods—especially traditional textbook teaching?

This is a process I suggest parents take their time with. One way to ease into the Charlotte Mason method is to not make any sudden changes until you're comfortable. To accomplish a smooth transition you could continue using your textbooks full time and begin to augment them with whole books and living books, such as biographies, autobiographies or well written historical novels. History is probably an excellent subject to experiment with to see how the Charlotte Mason method works for your family.

Some home schoolers live in states that insist upon maintaining proper grade level and legally they demand the parents provide ample proof through testing mechanisms that the local school authorities actually review. Because each state has different laws, and for many other reasons, I would not ask parents to give up anything they're depending on for security.

I can tell you that as you begin to augment with Charlotte Mason techniques you will probably react like so many other parents have and see how much more education is occurring for you and your children. You'll also see which part of your home schooling day is the most enjoyed and the most anticipated.

If you've already reached this point then the next Charlotte Mason item to add would be narration. Once narration is understood and applied to your children's education, then the difference in quality of narrations from textbooks compared to living books will no doubt strike you as very obvious. You'll find children who read one well-written book that revolves around one topic retain more information than those who read textbooks that try to cover too much at once. The passages in textbooks tend to be very short on any given person or event. In a whole book or living book method the end result will be retained knowledge.

Another way to make slow changes is to use whatever method you ordinarily use most of the week and save a little time one afternoon a week to try one new Charlotte Mason concept at a time. You can then devote portions of your seasonal breaks, such as summer, to further experiment with this method. Adding some art study or poetry reading could be another way to test the waters. After doing this type of experimentation myself, what occurred in my home was overwhelming. The difference in methods quickly became evident, and the choice became clear for our family.

We have referred back to our textbook collection because they serve as quick reminders of what topics others are studying. One year we looked at both a fifth-grade science and a fifth-grade history book to help formulate a year-long plan. After choosing some topics we made our living book choices so that they would correspond to both subjects. Because we covered mammals in science and we were studying English history our literature choice was *Black Beauty*. Some days we read from both the textbooks and the living books but it was continually apparent that the narrations from the textbooks were not beneficial. Keeping in mind that children can only narrate what they know, and they were skilled at narrating, I knew the fault was in the textbooks. As usual the passages were too short and general to receive any real knowledge.

It is a common opinion that textbooks rely on spiraling (covering) the same topics year after year hoping to build on the data from previous years. Many home school parents have become frustrated with this approach and have already substituted it with unit studies. It is your choice—do you want to study frogs a little in third grade, fourth and a little more in fifth? Possibly frogs will come up again in junior high during an amphibian chapter. The grand finale will probably be to dissect a frog in high school. My time is valuable to me and I would prefer to cover frogs once and really cover the topic well.

Currently, it is rare for us to use our textbooks because we've collected whole books that cover our material better, and the enthusiasm and quality of the narrations is always greatly improved. We've kept the textbooks in order to use them as we would any reference tool.

Another way to run a combination school, is to master a few of Charlotte's techniques but continue to use textbooks in some subjects. When you're more familiar and comfortable with the way she teaches spelling, for example, then you could drop that textbook. The occasional use of workbooks by even a full-time Charlotte Mason home is not forbidden. There are benefits to the teacher—they can be time-savers. Some children like workbooks, and if they are not "done to death" in a home, the children may continue to like them. As I said in my first book, my opinion is every child should learn how to use a textbook and how to receive an "A" from a course taught that way in the event they ever attend a class not conducted by Mason's method.

You will find that the more you know about Charlotte's methods, the more the textbooks will leave you lacking. She is concerned with "ideas" in contrast with learning just facts. She wants children to love to learn, and this is accomplished by providing the most interesting material possible. She wrote in *A Philosophy of Education,* "We should probably be more scientific as a people if we scrapped all the textbooks." (p. 218) I know from personal experience that finding science books that are interesting and of a literary quality is a challenge. This is one of the tasks (if you want to call it that) of following this method. It means always being on the lookout for possible books and becoming skilled at assessing them at a moment's notice.

How do you get started with a limited budget? Home schooling is so expensive, do you have any money saving ideas?

People on a budget (whether it's because they have to be or because they are pursuing a simpler way of life for other reasons) tend to do very well at cutting corners and doing without unnecessary expenditures—until it comes to home education. Some bargain-minded folks are very savvy about shipping rates and discount catalog companies and still the spending goes on and on. Why? Because money spent on our deserving children can be easily justified especially when it goes for educational books, games, calendars, videos and computer gadgets.

Erasmus said, "When I get a little money I buy books and if any is left I buy food and clothes." That could certainly describe some of my book loving friends and because books are vital to education we need to know when to cut corners and when not to. There was a time when books were so expensive that schools could not use them. The lecture system of classroom education came from that situation—the teacher had to convey his knowledge to the students without any books. Thankfully, that day is gone!

One of my favorite aspects of the Charlotte Mason method is the fact that it can be done very economically and there isn't expensive curriculum to purchase. For the most part, the books you use in any method of home schooling can be obtained from the library at no charge, which is the most economical source for all kinds of books. Incidentally, my ideal library would be a place where we could check out resources (such as microscopes) and educational tools and our privileges would not be limited to printed matter. If you agree, let your local lawmaker know that you'd approve of your library expanding its stock to include more hands-on learning tools. Even though it would come out of your taxes, in the long run, it may prove more economical to share than to have each household owning its own microscope.

If you find yourself thinking, "But I need curriculum not books!" The truth is you need both. The library has biographies, poetry, huge coffee table size art appreciation books and they have periodicals on bird watching, sewing, gardening—anything you can think of is available.

In-between library visits you'll want to frequent garage sales, used bookstores and large thrift stores, keeping your eyes open for interesting books on educational topics and classic literature. While you're looking keep in mind to be well read is to be well educated. Because it's difficult to read an entire classic during a library loan (even with renewals) you'll want to start an inexpensive collection of them. One book per payday is how I managed to obtain a rather large collection. When buying an inexpensive book always look for a readable format. You want it to open comfortably and have a good, wide margin so that the text does not run into the spine of the book. Nobody will enjoy reading a book that was not constructed properly and if no one reads it, you've wasted your money. Bantam Books has a wonderful series of classics in paperback form.

Home schooling families are often on a limited budget due to the one income lifestyle they have chosen. It is usually a necessity to have one parent available to teach the children. So when you find the money for books is scarce, think on the bright side. Your collection will reflect the fact that you had to be more choosy concerning your purchases. Fewer books, but excellently written books, is something to be proud of.

Thrift stores sell used books and much of yesterday's textbooks have landed in the used book departments in all kinds of stores. Many of them are terrible. They stink, have missing pages and even in their prime they weren't worth owning. But, just like digging through piles of used clothing will result in one wearable garment, educational books are worth looking for, and you have to be every bit as discriminating.

You will find non-consumable spelling and math books. Quite often they are reference tools that for twenty–five to fifty–cents will enable you to instantly turn to the formula, mathematical concept, spelling rule, etc. you need to refresh yourself on. Incidentally, non-consumable products, whether new or used, are always the best bargain. The can be used by all the children in your own home and they sell well as used curriculum.

Old history textbooks are also available. Again, you'll come across bad examples of yesterday's schooling and make sure you do not buy anything that you find to be boring. Pick up each book and look past its cover and layout (and sometimes its smell) and look carefully at several different written sections. You want the writing to grab you and make you want to know more of what the book is saying. If that is not your reaction, chances are the book is boring.

You'll find the selection of biographies to be endless. Biographies provide a birds-eye-view into a person's life, and don't be fooled, you'll learn a lot more than just one person's life. Benjamin Franklin's autobiography is a good example of this. When I read it and enjoyed every minute of it (which, by the way, is a very cheap form of entertainment) I learned that he did not like paperback books but it was all he could afford when he was a young man. That was news to me—that the United States had paperback books so long ago. That's one way my knowledge about our country, its economics and daily life were expanded upon for me. Franklin spent some time in Europe which he also wrote about. Had he elaborated much upon that continent who knows what else I could have picked up that I would not have otherwise learned.

Another school subject available at the used book stores and in antique stores is art. There are inexpensive prints and art books galore. I'm not sure you can collect too much beautiful artwork to have on-hand for your family's enjoyment, for school and to enhance the home.

At this point you may be wondering if I ever recommend buying new curriculum. Not if there's an alternative. When curriculum is needed try buying it used whenever possible. The next best thing to free is cheap. So where is the cheap used curriculum? It's usually at the used curriculum sale that large home school support groups host once a year. Prices range from twenty–five cents for a partially used workbook to half-price of the current catalog price. The best way to present a used workbook for sale is to rip out the used pages. Then your customer will open the cover and see immediately where the book picks up the topic. Maybe her child just got to fraction division and at a glance she can see your used math book "starts" with that. Of course non-consumable material will not have been consumed in any manner and it makes a very good purchase or sell. If no one has a used sale in your town, hold one yourself. Find a free room and charge each person $1.00 dollar admittance. Also charge each "vendor" $1.00 for a table. Then you'll have a little money to offset your expenses but it won't appear that your motive was to make money.

Selling curriculum to one another at your support group is another option. Let people know you're ready to unload your sixth grade stuff now that your child is going into seventh grade. Hopefully, that will become a habit among the group.

There are retail stores whose entire stock is used curriculum. There could be countless hundreds of these stores across the country. The greater Seattle area has one called Titus Women's Homeschool Potpourri. The phone number is 425-820-4626. You can sell your old stuff and/or tell the owner what you're in the market for.

Many of the big curriculum exhibitions offer a used sale either the day before, a few hours before, or rarely, concurrently with the new item booths. If you've wondered why they often keep them separate it's to please the vendors of new curriculum. Their sales suffer if you're able to buy their products in an adjacent room for half price. I understand vendors have high overhead and other expenses and I do wish them well—but I sympathize with the need of the home school parent to economize.

Another way the home schooling support groups can help is by providing us an avenue to "show and tell." Actually seeing products helps us to save money because we'll often find they are not really what we're looking for. The reverse is also true—you can see something that would work perfectly for your child. Encourage your support group leader to start a show and tell segment in each meeting, every other meeting or a few select meetings per year.

Have participants bring the materials they use and talk about them. Sometimes new items have more hype about them than is justified. When you can see the curriculum up close and examine it for yourself you'll save yourself a lot of money. Sometime support groups have libraries that everybody can borrow from. If that's not possible try co-owning books with friends.

I want to provide two quotes that are meant to inspire you. Willingham F. Rawnsley, who thought very highly of Charlotte Mason wrote, "It is books and more books that the children must have, both prose and poetry by good authors who have the power of writing clearly and in good English and have something interesting to say." Charlotte Mason said, "We believe that most parents of children in the [C. Mason home schools] feel that it would be better to do without many things than without the best books, various books, and fresh books for the children's studies. As a matter of fact, the difference between educated and uneducated people is that the former know and love books; the latter may have passed examinations."

How can we identify "twaddle" and prevent our children from reading it?

Because Charlotte Mason strongly recommended the avoidance of twaddle, parents are often concerned about what it is and how they can successfully avoid it. Synonyms of twaddle include, babble, drivel and silly.

There are many series that are written for children which I think represent twaddle and one sensible step is to not introduce the family to them. Instead, become an expert on spotting genuine literature and avoid the counterfeit, much like the training that a bank teller receives.

A review of what Charlotte would want us to look for in a book would include well-constructed sentences clothed in literary language. She wanted the imagination to be warmed and the book to hold the interest of the child. Also keep in mind her opinion that life is too short to spend time with books that bore us. If we can find an interesting book and a boring book on the same topic then it is obvious which one we should choose.

Unfortunately, we live in a "dumbed-down" society, and all around us is the evidence of it. For example, it has been said that our current newspapers are now written at a seventh-grade reading level. Also, there is a noticeably different atmosphere in our schools all the way up to the college level. The workload in college has dramatically *decreased*, and "A" and "B" grades are being given to today's students for work that may not have even been deemed passing ten or twenty years ago. Dumbed-down information is prevalent in most of our modern writings, even in the forms we fill out. Let's help combat this by improving the literary taste of the next generation.

If our children have only been exposed to junk food, they may resist trying nutritious food. If they have been raised on twaddle, they may need to be weaned slowly off of this mental junk food.

It is my opinion that dumbed-down literature is easy to spot. When you are standing in the library and pick up modern-day, elementary-level books, you are apt to see short sentences with very little effort applied to artistically constructing them to please the mind. Almost anyone can write—but not everyone is gifted in this field. Gifted authors bring images alive with their choice of words. (I do not claim to be gifted in this area, by the way. Writing is just an efficient mode of communication to me—I much prefer talking.) Gifted authors often write classic literature and classics are an excellent way to spend one's reading time.

Twaddle is easy to come by; the planet is filled with it. People coped with it in Charlotte Mason's day, and we must cope with it in ours. If anything, literature has deteriorated even further. The best way to cope with this excessive quantity of bad books is to stand firm and only spend our money on the best.

But that's us, the parents, learning a skill. How do we help others like friends and relatives to understand so that they aren't supplying our children with twaddle at gift-giving times? We need to talk to them about the direction our families have taken. Perhaps, we need to explain and be able to defend our home schooling philosophy to our friends, relatives and even our critics. Some people pick up on things easier than others, therefore, for some well-meaning folks a simple explanation of the type of literature that you want purchased as gifts is all they need. If you have started to collect any particular set of children's classics that are currently in bookstores or available through catalogs, you could provide Grandma with a list of titles you'd like. Be specific, and offer to help her with the ordering or perhaps even drive her to your favorite bookstore.

What is drilling?

I have found that Charlotte Mason parents are very curious about drilling and it has been an extremely frequent question. When I wrote *A Charlotte Mason Education* I was using the designated time for drilling as the portion of our week when we would memorize things like the American presidents, the kings and queens of England, the alphabet, phonics, roman numerals, multiplication table, the names of the states, countries, continents, oceans and the constellations. Either I created homemade charts or I purchased them at teacher stores. I have found them to be very effective and they cover many topics. We have a chart naming the most common underwater creatures, another of the human skeleton, the parts of speech and when to use a capital letter. Literally, *anything* I want my children to remember by rote I post on the wall and we drill it. However, this is not what Charlotte Mason was talking about when she referred to drill. In her schedules, drilling was time allowed for exercise; or we may think of it as calisthenics. The closest I have come to applying her concept of drill is letting my children out in the backyard during school to refresh their minds and interest before tackling another subject.

Math

There are always a lot of questions regarding math. Parents frequently ask how the short lessons works with math, which math books to purchase and occasionally the questions describe an attitude problem on the part of the child.

Let's approach the attitude problem first. Mainly, I've heard of children complaining, moping, dawdling and even groaning. Children will groan. When one of mine got into the habit of a mellow-dramatic death scene each time the math books needed to be retrieved, I realized I had better do something about it.

I used Charlotte Mason's suggestion of appealing to the child's sense of right. I simply asked my grade school aged daughter if she thought groaning was the right reaction when she was informed that it was math time. Her face immediately changed, and I saw that my point (Charlotte's point) had registered. Her attitude problem ended then and there and I am happy to report that two years later she is still exhibiting a good attitude at math time. Why did this work out so well for me? Because the power of habit is just that—powerful.

If complaining has become habitual in your home the first step is to recognize that it is indeed a habit. Charlotte's teaching on habits is a very profitable one to become acquainted with and is dealt with in *Home Education* pages 119 to 168, or the condensed account in my book, *A Charlotte Mason Education*.

Sometimes it's Mom who gets into bad habits. I had read, understood and practiced Charlotte's teachings on math, but when it was time to work with my one of my younger children I found myself with a problem. This particular child enjoyed preschool and kindergarten math workbooks so I let her use them. After going through more of those than I can count, I knew the time had come to move on to a first-grade math book. She didn't find this as fun. She was puzzled, and I was frightened even though she was my fourth (out of five) home schooling student. Fortunately, someone came along and asked my opinion of Charlotte Mason's teachings on math with this age group. That brought back better memories for me of working with this student. Compared with the workbook struggle we were in, those seemed like pleasant days. Rereading the math section in *Home Education* (Vol. 1, pgs. 253–264) turned out to be the best prescription for our ailment. (Also see the math chapter in *A Charlotte Mason Education*.)

I hadn't realized that I had fallen into the workbook rut and into the habit of relying on it. The next day at math time, which started with the usual sadness, I got out the counters, (dried beans and buttons) and we did some math problems with them. It was like playing a game with each other, and she had genuine joy on her face. The most amazing thing about it was that I discovered her math knowledge was considerably more advanced than I knew.

Further solutions for an attitude problem include using proper motivations to your advantage and the use of short lessons, both of which are covered in the short lessons chapter of this book. A short lesson usually works for developing the power of attention and is also an excellent tool to use for subjects that are not enjoyable. Knowing that math will only last for fifteen minutes today and will not be asked of the student again until tomorrow is a great motivation. (Don't overlook the fact that the allotted math time changes to thirty minutes during junior high and to forty–five minutes during high school and they were based on a six day school week.) Short lessons serve as an incentive because the idea of going from something the child doesn't like to something he does like in a fifteen minute interval usually helps the child to persevere.

Some mothers have mentioned to me that their husbands are not in favor of applying short lessons in the area of math. I would not hesitate to invite dad to participate in the math instruction by possibly adding an additional fifteen (or thirty, or forty–five) minutes of math each evening so he can personally supervise the progress of each student. This way the benefits of short concentrated efforts toward math are not lost. If your husband is *really* against the concept and that does not pacify him, invite him to conduct a "long" lesson with the children each evening. And lastly, if it's a long lesson he'd like the children to have and he does not want to participate then by all means keep the peace and teach a long math lesson to your children on a daily basis—neither of you will be the worse for it, but it will take time away from other profitable subjects.

As to the ever popular question of what math curriculum I use and recommend, I have not yet found a Charlotte Mason math book on the market. That only leaves me with one option—I have had to adapt every math book I've used to the Charlotte Mason method. Each of you has the same dilemma. Do you buy a math book and use it as it was designed or do you alter it until it fits with your philosophy?

Technically, if you wanted to follow C. Mason's advice with the younger grade levels, and really wanted to apply yourself to her strategies, you could forgo the purchasing of math workbooks. It would mean using manipulatives such as pebbles and buttons, giving the children *lots* of oral "story" problems, and you would need to write your own math problems on paper or on your white board. I briefly tried this but like trying to write your own handwriting course it takes a lot of time. Instead, I would use a workbook or textbook but not become enslaved to it. In the last ten years I've used many different types of books and I'm not partial to any one company. Even when I think I have developed a favorite I find it necessary to switch "brands" because I don't like to use one book over and over again.

One truly original math book I like is called *Grocery Cart Math* by Jaye Hansen. At first glance I thought I could do the ideas given in the book without buying it. As I spent more time with it I realized I wouldn't follow through on the ideas if I didn't own and use the book routinely. The concept is to take the book with you to the store and fill in the blanks, but it is not another boring workbook. It's appropriate for use during the mid-elementary grades and should be used concurrently with any standard math curriculum—not in place of one. You'll find it necessary to keep it in the car—or you'll find "out of sight out of mind" is a very true axiom.

I have a great deal of Saxon math books on hand—because they're available I use them. Again, I had to choose whether to follow Mr. Saxon's guidelines which concentrate on not skipping any problems or to disregard his advice and follow Charlotte's short lesson concept instead.

With grade school and junior high level students I found it fairly easy to skip problems and help the child to work independently by taking the math book to my computer and quickly preparing two weeks' worth of math lessons from it. In the case of Saxon books I look at the new teaching offered for the day and decide if we need to cover it or not. I can always tell which concepts my children are going to need me to teach and which they will be independent with, because I know them and how they think. Then I quickly look at the practice problems that go with the new teaching and decide if they are necessary or not. I then judge which problems from the review set seem important with the short lesson amount of time in mind. About a third of the time we are able to disregard the new teaching in a Saxon book because it's either redundant or the topic seems unnecessary to cover at this time. If I skip the new teaching for the day, I only choose problems from the review set and I try to choose problems that are similar. I can either post these assignments on the wall, and the child crosses them out as they are completed or they could be written in a day planner book. Either way, this method helps the child to become less dependent.

When a new math concept is introduced that one of my children cannot learn from the book, I favor teaching the new concept to that child on a non-school day. Rarely can I teach a new concept to any of them during the school week, unless everyone is being unusually cooperative that particular day. (Remember, I have a large family—this would not apply to situations where one or two children are present.) Much of the time then, the daily short lessons are used for math practice. Week by week a parent could teach the children all of the necessary concepts they need to learn in any given grade and only purchase drill books to be used for practice during the daily short lesson time.

Several years ago when my former high school student used the Saxon Algebra I book, I did not opt for short lessons. She completed the entire lesson as designed by Saxon. I noticed the lessons took about two hours to complete. She went through that book twice, and even the second time, it did *not* cut down the length of time per lesson. Until someone writes a math curriculum with short lessons in mind we'll have to continue to choose from two options—adapt the book or decide not to follow the Charlotte's advice in this particular area. You may find your decisions differing from child to child, especially if one of them enjoys math and asks to work in his book for a longer time period. That's the kind of person who might choose to major in a mathematical field in college.

I was encouraged to have a representative from the Saxon company attend one of my Charlotte Mason seminars. He was serving as a consultant for an upcoming revision of the entire line of books. I was pleased with his curiosity of the Charlotte's method and he asked me in what ways I would change the books. Happily, I answered his questions and we can only hope that Charlotte Mason's influence will make some kind of mark.

Finding a literary math book is next to impossible but the closest thing you'll probably find is a biography of a mathematician's life. If you don't already have one you might want to look for one at the used book store. There are a couple of readily available books that briefly cover thirty of the mathematician's lives called *Mathematicians are People, Too—Stories from the Lives of Great Mathematicians*. There are two volumes in the set, and they're written by Luetta and Wilbert Reimer. Each book covers fifteen mathematicians including their discovery. Their life spans begin at 636 B.C. with the closest to modern times being A.D. 1985. While it is not an in-depth view into these historical people, it is a very nice treat to add to a math curriculum for students between first and eighth grade.

We struggle with poetry. What are we doing wrong?

Poetry can grow on you—if at first you don't care for it keep trying. I'm grateful for my first exposure because it came so early in my life. It took place during one of many times I had an extended illness as a child. My mother brought me a copy of Robert Louis Stevenson's *A Child's Garden of Verses*. She explained to me that he was a sickly child and maybe I'd be able to relate to his childhood.

Since writing the chapter on poetry in my first book I've greatly increased the amount of time the children and I spend with it—both in leisure time and during school time. It has become a very important part of our lives. Check the schedules in the appendix—you'll see we increased to four times a week of reading, memorizing and reciting poetry.

A quick review of how we teach poetry in the Charlotte Mason method includes the foremost goal—enjoy it. It was written to be enjoyed with a possible secondary purpose of thought provocation.

If you and the kids are not enjoying yourselves keep trying! For some it's an acquired taste like coffee. Maybe you haven't found the right poetry or poet. When children struggle with narrations, often the breakthrough occurs when they come across the "right" book for them. I believe it's similar with this topic. Eventually you'll find something they like.

Charlotte Mason thought it was a very good idea to have children memorize poems. She taught that the adult could read the poem while the child was occupied with something else and even if they weren't concentrating they would still be able to memorize it. She opted to forego the full concentration she usually advocated.

At our house we approach it differently. I have the children pay full attention while they're working on a poem but I do not make it weary for them. Once a poem is selected for memorization I type a copy for them to use and I save it in the poetry file in my computer. Filing them this way helps to keep a record and younger children can use the same poem when they arrive at the same age. Also, when they're on file they can be printed and used for handwriting practice.

At recitation time each child gets their poem and reads it through to themselves a couple of times. After that they turn to the rest of us and recite as much as they know. Children have good memories and they are capable of memorizing quickly. I've never had one single complaint about it. On the contrary they are quite pleased with themselves when they finish a poem.

If you are receiving complaints about poetry reading even after trying a variety of poetry then try these ideas. Read the poem but *do not read the title*. Have the kids guess what the poem was about—quite often the answer is the same as the title. There are *a lot of poems that work for this*. It does not take prior preparation. Just skim the poem quickly checking to see if the title of the poem is ever mentioned. The children love this and it makes the activity less passive.

Try acting out the poem. *Three Little Kittens* and *Puppy and I* are good ones to start with. You take a speaking part like mother cat and assign parts to the kids. Tell them what their line will be and you'll be amazed at how quick they memorize it. They like physically acting out the poem during the reading whether they have a line or not. This idea is strictly for young children—I don't suggest it for high school.

Another reason some don't enjoy poetry is they are spending time comparing, criticizing, dissecting, analyzing or they're counting the beats per line. Icky! People don't like to do this. Poets don't like it when we do this. Alexander Pope (1688–1744) wrote a huge, amusing poem on criticism entitled *An Essay on Criticism*. I highly recommend you read it if you doubt poets dread these practices.

Poetry does not take preparation time on your part. Maybe you're avoiding it because you've come to think of it as work. During poetry reading time I read poetry. I never, repeat never, choose selections ahead of time. It's fun to grab an anthology and read at random. The fact that people make connections on their own is proven to be true again when you do this. Life just *is* connected.

Even random reading will bring about poems that one of my children has memorized before. You'd think they were in heaven when this happens. It makes them happy to recite it along with me. In fact everybody recites it because when one of them memorizes a poem, trust me, we all become familiar with it.

My best advice is to have one good anthology handy, right where you home school. Then you'll include poetry. If there isn't poetry around you won't.

What's the best way to run a Charlotte Mason support group?

Of course there is no one right way to do anything. I have experience running a group and I've discussed the matter with many other leaders. Everybody approaches it differently. I believe I'm partial to a low-key home group because it fosters support. However, the one I led could not have been more different.

One of the reasons our group had such large attendance was due to the publicity. When I decided it was worth starting, I thought there would be three of four of us attending. That was perfectly fine with me, however, I did put the word out because for a long time I had felt like the only home schooling person using the Charlotte Mason method in the entire state. It had felt very lonely and I decided not to run a group without letting others know. I couldn't bear the thought of someone like myself living nearby without any knowledge of the meeting. It was not my intention to make Charlotte Mason converts but I knew I would have been willing to drive a distance to attend a meeting like this, had there been one. The moral is if you want a small group don't advertise. Large groups are fun but not as supportive.

Another reason our group could grow was the room we used. I chose a public meeting room at the library because I didn't want to make my family leave home during the meetings and I didn't want to "stress out" about the entertaining aspect of having people over. The library room sat ninety and it's a good thing it did. It was always a crowded meeting with parents driving from all four compass points—from up to two hours away.

Prior to the first meeting there was a sign up sheet sent around a small local group to see who was interested. I guess that should have been my first indication, everyone there signed it. I wanted to know their names but I also wanted to know which night of week would *not* work for them, they each noted one. That resulted in only one day in common, Sunday. In that town the Sunday night church service was almost nonexistent.

The good thing about Sunday was the lack of traffic. Recently, I was told that Seattle is the next in line for traffic problems after Los Angeles. On a week night those two hour car trips could have doubled and that alone would have prevented people from coming. The bad thing about Sunday nights was having to explain them. The best rationalization was every time the group was polled about the night of the week they preferred and whether they had a better idea, Sunday was chosen over and over again. Also, we only met four times a year. If someone had to choose between a church service and the meeting it was a personal choice and many would send Dad and kids off to church without them.

There had been some serious and heartbreaking leadership struggles in my county previous to my becoming a leader. I asked around and found a common thread to the problem. Apparently, having a board provides a potential situation for the leader to be voted out of leadership. The solution to that problem is never to form one in the first place. I ran my Charlotte Mason group as a friendly dictator, however, I gave the participants surveys on a continuous basis so I was able to know what they wanted. I've found this to be the best way to please a group of people. I'm happy to say that we never encountered disputes, hard feelings or bickering of any kind.

Not having a board does not mean you have to do without help. People always arrived early and stayed late to set up and tear down. Originally, I called down the list to find three or four people to bring snack and drink to each meeting. Food really helped the atmosphere of the room which was a little sterile. Eventually, I found someone willing to be snack coordinator and she did the organizing. We always had snack first to give the group something to do while tardy people found their way to a seat. I brought a compact disc player and had music playing for the first fifteen minutes until I officially started the meeting. It helped create an inviting atmosphere.

Someone also volunteered to be treasurer, but we did not charge money to attend the group. We did collect offerings to offset the cost of hand-outs and we had a separate fund for the lending library. The treasurer bought many Charlotte Mason-type books that people could borrow. During our final meeting we drew the names of the books from a hat until all of the items had been dispersed back to the people who had funded them. The treasurer kept track of costs with receipts and reported how far we were in the hole each meeting. At anytime the decision could have been made to charge a membership fee of twenty or so dollars per year; however, I continually opted to have a free group. During one meeting we were able to raise a large sum of money for two needy families attending the group and I was able to keep their identities secret.

The meetings were highly structured and each minute accounted for. With people driving from so far away I did not want any dead-air time. People enjoyed the organization and it was constantly complimented.

After snack we would have announcements and show-and-tell. Anyone could bring something they wanted to share with others and people would announce free classical music concerts or plays that were upcoming.

Before any new teaching I would ask how the group had *implemented* last meeting's teachings. Usually there was time to ask other provocative questions such as what in the Charlotte Mason method was working best for them, if anything was hindering their home schooling at the present time or how to challenge our children's minds. They were asked questions about the group such as what they would have liked to see in a newcomer packet, if they wanted an annual picnic or if they wanted to organize an activity for our children.

At several meetings we broke into four groups and went to the four corners in order to foster relationships and support. I would supply them with interesting topics with the hope they would have plenty to talk about. Occasionally we tried to have people sit according to the city they lived in hoping they would find friends and carpools.

From the first meeting on I used ten-minute teachers. I was apprehensive of setting myself up as the only teacher because I saw there would be no escape from the role. I wanted everyone at the same level and I knew if people were interested in a topic they would enjoy researching and teaching it. I would send around two sign up sheets every meeting, one for snack and one for teachers. If the list for teachers came back blank I would send it around again. It worked well to circulate it after someone had given a great teaching and made it look easy.

We would have two or three of the ten-minute teachings, per meeting, all on different topics. Before the first meeting I created a huge list of Charlotte Mason topics and then surveyed the group as to which they wanted first. We used that list and we had completed most of them when I chose to end the group.

Early during the first year I became concerned that at the rate of two or three topics per meeting, with only four meetings a year, the participants would not get enough teaching to actually get them going in this method—at the time there were absolutely no Charlotte Mason books available on this method other than Susan Schaeffer Macaulay's. The six-volume set was back in print but it was difficult to enforce the purchase and the reading of them regardless of the many ways I sought to inspire people to participate in that way. I woke up one morning with the idea to give them a whole day of teaching on all of the school subjects, then we could keep meeting at the same rate and I wouldn't have to worry about their progress.

That turned out to be a more ambitious undertaking than I could have known. I gave myself five months to prepare, research and practice. Teaching others how to use the Charlotte Mason method proved to be challenging. Charlotte's writings focus on the philosophical aspects but I wanted to provide practical information in an easy to understand all-day seminar. I did not want to teach parents techniques that I had not actually used with my children—that way I could make certain the teaching would be useful and valid. Because I didn't charge any money many of the state home schooling newsletters publicized the event for me at no cost. Later the teaching I gave that day became my first book.

During the support group meetings I always took one of the teachings and I always went last. That way if time was short I could still end the meeting on time which I did consistently—it's the only polite thing to do on a Sunday night when people have a long drive ahead of them.

Small, regional support groups were encouraged from the beginning. I kept a list of people who were interested in attending, hosting or leading a group in their town. I introduced people to one another and shared phone numbers in an effort to coordinate a meeting in many of Seattle's suburbs. I wanted people to have living room groups in their area so that attending our "big meeting" could become an occasional excursion and they would not have to depend upon it. We had plenty of people from our own area to keep our attendance high.

Hosting and leading are separate skills and they do not need be to resident in the same person. Once someone with the graciousness to open their home to others is found, then a leader can commute to the meeting. It is necessary to have someone with natural leadership skills guide the meeting, even if it's small. Good leaders are not overly talk-ative, bossy or controlling. They tend to be naturally charismatic which is helpful because you want people to gravitate around one central per-son and theme in order to have a successful group. Diplomacy is also a crucial trait because sooner or later unproductive topics or even debates will emerge. Good leaders are born with the ability to bring a group back to the appropriate topic without offending anyone. In the absence of a leader one will emerge from any group of people. If a person with-out these skills attempts to lead a meeting she risks having someone from the group itself feeling as though they must "help" her. Of course people with leadership skills attend meetings all the time that they do not lead. They have to squelch their tendency to guide a group whether it is faltering or not. They must learn to remain quiet when they attend other's meetings.

Another key to success in any meeting or organization is to know *why* you're meeting. Some Charlotte Mason groups only discuss Char-lotte Mason—others allow various topics. Some set out with a combina-tion in mind such as Charlotte Mason and classical education.

Following is the list of topics we covered in our group in the order we presented them. I taught fourteen of them, volunteers taught the rest. Narration, the Child Light Series, nature notebooks, the formation of habit, enjoying our families, how to use short lessons, how to occupy preschoolers, formation of character, developing good literary taste, how to replace workbooks, yearly examinations, artists, art study, Charlotte Mason on-line, book of centuries, children and free time, the liberal arts, I am I can I ought I will, astronomy, trimester planning, music, musicians, using the Bible in school, Charlotte Mason Sunday Schools, how to play charades with children, moral training for children, poetry, foreign languages, language arts, visiting museums in Italy, how to select books, how to plan a school year and high school.

These meetings were immensely popular and well attended. Many times I was told how closely guarded the meeting dates were on people's calendars. They would swear nothing could come between them and their meeting. I did take that as a compliment but it was also human nature to look forward to a meeting that only comes a few times a year. I enjoyed each and every meeting and will always look back at them with fondness. Leading a group does take a lot of work and dedication. If ever you find yourself with the opportunity, strongly consider taking it. It may be one of the most rewarding things you'll ever do. I'm grateful to my former group for coming and making all the work more than worthwhile.

FOURTEEN

For Further Study

$\mathscr{I}$needed a very powerful reason to write a second book because I still feel strongly that reading Charlotte Mason's books would be the most beneficial use of your time. However, with both books I've tried to help the home schooling parents and other educators with the practical, daily, "how-to" of this incredibly valuable method. My intention was to give you enough information so that you could actually implement the method in your home. Then, you could read and reread Charlotte Mason's books at your leisure, hopefully without so much pressure to interpret her meaning in order to start application.

Some people find Charlotte Mason's six-volume set to be difficult reading and many have found it to be a four to five year long project. I don't mean to discourage you from trying to read it, on the contrary I want to help you to succeed at it. You can read *from* the set if you're not able to read through it. I'm providing my advice as to how to tackle the six-volumes because I can't even count the number of people who have told me that they own the set, they've attempted to read it, but they neither enjoy nor understand it. Let me reassure you—you *can* read Charlotte Mason's books.

How to read the six-volume set

ACCEPT NO SUBSTITUTES
- When possible, go to Charlotte Mason's materials directly. People have and will continue to misconstrue her ideas. We all approach this method with our own thoughts and biases on education. As we read, we tend to take an idea and make it our own for our children. If you know what Charlotte Mason said, you'll be able to recognize when an author has applied her writings verbatim or adapted her ideas.
- Take notes when you read.
- Keep a notepad with your books and do not neglect to write down ideas or examples. (Do this enough and you'll be writing your own book on the Charlotte Mason method!)
- Get alone in a quiet place.
- As many of you have found, this is not light reading. Prepare to concentrate and think. Countless times I could have taken Charlotte's meaning the wrong way. It truly takes concentration.

PRIORITIZE YOUR READING
If time is a limitation, concentrate your efforts on the three volumes that end in the word "education." *Home Education, School Education* and *Philosophy of Education.*

EXPECT TO REREAD
This includes sentences, paragraphs and entire books in the series. Even if you've developed the ability to grasp written content in one reading, she has so much to say about so many things that it can be difficult to grasp it all in one reading. Plus, as we and our children grow older the potential for seeing her teachings in a whole new way expands at each plateau.

In addition to Charlotte Mason's works there are many books written about her and her methods. Most of us are familiar with *For the*

Children's Sake, written by Susan Schaeffer Macaulay in the mid 1980's. But, are you aware of Jenny King's *Charlotte Mason Reviewed* written in 1981? Evidently, it is hard to come by so if you ever get the opportunity to buy it or read it don't pass it up—I've read my copy several times. It was published in England and you'll find it to be very accurate—Charlotte Mason's ideas come through as if she herself was condensing the philosophies. It will be a particularly helpful book for the classroom teacher.

Some of you may have obtained through interlibrary loan, *The Story of Charlotte Mason* by Essex Cholmondeley since my recommendation in my first book. She also wrote *Parents are Peacemakers* published in 1944. In addition there is *In Memoriam of Charlotte M. Mason* published by the PNEU in 1923. This is the most touching book as those who knew her recalled the details that made her not only a beautiful person but one who led such an influential life.

Also available through interlibrary loan is a biography of Henrietta Franklin (a key person in Charlotte's life and work) called *Netta* by Monk Gibbon. Mrs. Franklin was a little more than twenty years younger than Charlotte Mason and met her as a published educationalist when Charlotte was in her early fifties. *Netta* is a well written 253 page book and was published in 1960. While it is Franklin's biography and not Mason's, it is a great inside look at the work of the PNEU and as one of Charlotte's closest friends it's an interesting view of their relationship. Also, Franklin herself wrote, *The Home Training of Children* in 1908, a book I have not had the pleasure of reading.

You may remember another of Charlotte's friends, Dr. Helen Webb—she published articles in Charlotte Mason's magazine the *Parents' Review*. A collection of those articles are available in a book titled, *Children and the Stress of Life*. The chapter titles are; Formation of Habit, On One Aspect of Nursery Hygiene, The Stress of Life, A Nursery Talk, On Thought-Turning as a Factor in the Training of Character, Why Small Things Matter, Early Influences, The Child as a Person, Seed Time and Unchartered Freedom. One of my first encounters with other

Charlotte Mason enthusiasts took place many years ago at a Charlotte Mason school. That afternoon we were treated to a very edifying lecture from this book. I think you'll find it contains very valuable direction.

The Term's Music by Cedric Howard Glover was published in 1925. This book was printed for the Parents' Union School for their use term by term and also appeared as articles in Charlotte Mason's *Parents' Review*. One of the publishers is listed as J. Curwen & Sons, LTD, which is possibly a relative of Mrs. Curwen. This book covers four years of school by covering three composers per year (one composer per trimester). It includes other texts they read from and the pieces they played for the students. In the appendix are examination questions that cover the entire book. The composers covered are, Handel, Bach, Mozart, Beethoven, Schubert, Schumann, Brahms, Wagner, Grieg, Moussorgsky, Dvorak and Debussy.

There is a compilation of articles written by Eleanor Breckels (also known as Hilda Eleanor Breckels) called *Life in a PNEU Nursery School*. This work was written in the late 1960's and the 1970's. If you are interested in Charlotte Mason's ideals applied with the younger children you'll find this helpful and extensive. As with any out-of-print publication take your request to your librarian and ask her to search for it.

Four other resources are *A Liberal Education for All: Parents' Union School Prospectus, Specimen Programmes, suggestions, &c* (c 1920), by Charlotte Mason. This 25 page pamphlet has technical information which details the philosophy, the certificates, the home schoolrooms, the classes (grade levels), rules, fees and an entrance form to use if applying to the Parents' Union Schools (which were the home schools conducted in a correspondence style). Far more current is the *Charlotte Mason College* (1985) by J. P. Inman which is currently available from England by writing to: University College of St. Martin, Ambleside Campus, Rydal Road, Ambleside, Cumbria, LA22 9BB. This 88 page book has a lot of information about the Charlotte Mason College as it existed in Charlotte's day and then proceeds to detail the events following her death through to the mid 1980's. There are many pictures ranging from the 1880's to the 1980's. One image is the college badge that the students chose. It depicts rushes in the center with the words "For the Children's Sake" in the border. Thirdly, there is, *PNEU School: Independent Day School* published in May of 1987 by the World Wide Education Service of the PNEU. This brief booklet has many photographs, a well-done sketch of Charlotte Mason and the image of the skylark ascending that served as the children's badge. Apparently the author did much of her research from *The Story of Charlotte Mason*. You may be able to get a copy by writing to: 44-50 Osmaburgh Street, London, NW1 3NN. Also there is *Charlotte Mason—A Pioneer of Sane Education*, by Marian Wallace Ney. This book is from England and it was written in 1980 as part of Ney's college work and ultimately published in 1999. The ISBN is 190021914X. These four resources are great for those who *really* want as much information as they can get.

Charlotte Mason herself wrote two other six-volume sets. One is, *The Savior of the World*, in which she set the gospels to verse. Secondly, she wrote a set of English geography books. I have never had the privilege to see either of these sets with the exception of a few of the poems. Apparently the only location of the poetry for the United States is the Princeton Theological Seminary.

Charlotte's magazine the *Parents' Review* which continued several decades after her death is kept in the Library of Congress and in the National Library of Education. Charlotte edited it between 1890 and 1923. It was continued by colleagues and students until 1979. If you find yourself in Washington DC you can access the *Parents' Review* and make copies of articles. A valued acquaintance of mine has done just that. She untiringly made trips from the west coast as often as possible until she had been able to see all of the *Parents' Reviews* stored there (which is nearly all of them). She is a credit to the Charlotte Mason community as a dedicated researcher and I owe her my thanks for making available to me nearly all of the above mentioned resources.

May each of us enjoy our Charlotte Mason researching and experience fulfilling Charlotte Mason days.

To contact the author
or to schedule a speaking engagement,
write to Catherine Levison at:

———

CHARLOTTE MASON COMMUNIQUÉ-TIONS
PMB 500
2522 N. Proctor
Tacoma, WA 98406

Charlotte Mason's Weekly Schedule for the First–Third Grades

	M	T	W	TH	F	S
9:00– 9:20	Old Testament	New Testament	Writing	Old Testament	New Testament	Week's Work
9:20– 9:40	Printing	Drawing	Reading	Reading	Reading	Reading
9:40– 9:50	Repetition Poem	Repetition Parable	Continue Reading	Continue Reading	Repetition Hymn	Continue Reading
9:50–10:00	French	Picture Talk	French	French	Natural History	Object Lesson
10:00–10:20	Number	Handicrafts	Number	Handicrafts	Number	Number
10:20–10:35	Drill or	Sol-fa play	Drill or	French Song	Drill or	Sol-fa Play
10:35–10:50	Dancing		Dancing	Play	Dancing	
10:50–11:20	Reading	Number	Handicrafts	Writing and Brush-Drawing	Handicrafts	Writing and Brush Drawing
11:20–11:30	Natural History	Reading	Geography	Number	Geography	Natural History

Taken from Charlotte Mason's *Parents' Review,* December 1908

Charlotte Mason's Weekly Schedule for the Fourth–Sixth Grades

	M	T	W	TH	F	S
9:00- 9:20	Old Testament	New Testament	Natural History	Old Testament	New Testament	Week's Work
9:20- 9:50	Arithmetic	Arithmetic	English History	Arithmetic	Arithmetic	Arithmetic
9:50-10:20	Dictation	Natural History	Dictation	Grammar	Plutarch's Lives	Latin
10:20-10:50	Drill 10m. Play	German Song 10m. Play	Play 10m. Play	Drill 10m. Play	French Song 10m. Play	Drill
10:50-11:00	Repetition Poem	Repetition Bible	Repetition Bible	Repetition Poem	Dictation	Repetition Week's Work
11:00-11:20	Geography	English History	Geography	French History	Grammar	Nature Lore
11:20-12:00	French	Latin	French	Reading	German	French

Taken from Charlotte Mason's *Parents' Review*, December 1908

Charlotte Mason's Weekly Schedule for the Seventh–Eighth Grades

	M	T	W	TH	F	S
9:00- 9:20	Old Testament	New Testament	Natural History	Old Testament	New Testament	Physical Geography
9:20- 9:50	Arithmetic	German	Arithmetic	English Grammar	Euclid	Arithmetic
9:50-10:20	Dictation	Composition	Dictation	Reading	Greek or Roman Lives	Latin
10:20-10:50	Drill 10m. Play	German Song 10m. Play	Drill 10m. Play	French Song 10m. Play	Drill 10m. Play	Sol-fa 10m. Play
10:50-11:00	Repetition Poem	Repetition Bible (O.T.)	Repetition Euclid	Repetition Poem	Repetition Bible (N.T.)	Repetition Week's Work
11:00-11:20	Geography	English History	Latin	English History	English Grammar	Botany
11:20-11:30	Arithmetic (Mental)	Arithmetic (Mental)	Map Questions	Arithmetic (Mental)	Writing	Euclid
11:30-12:15	French	Latin	Italian	French	German	Italian
12:15- 1:00	Botany	Geology	French History	Physiology	Geography	English Grammar

Taken from Charlotte Mason's *Parents' Review*, December 1908

Charlotte Mason's Weekly Schedule for the Ninth Grade

	M	T	W	TH	F	S
9:00- 9:30	Old Testament	New Testament	Latin	Old Testament	New Testament	Physical Geography
9:30-10:00	Arithmetic	Euclid	French	Arithmetic	Euclid	Algebra
10:00-10:40	Geology	Composition	Literature	Astronomy	Every-day Morals	Latin
10:40-11:00	Drill Singing	Drill Singing	Drill Singing	Drill Singing	Drill Singing	Drill Singing
11:00-11:45	Literature	English History	Geography	English History	Grammar	Botany
11:45-12:15	Botany	Algebra	European History	Every-day Morals	Geography	Grammar
12:15- 1:00	French	German	Italian	French	German	Italian

Taken from Charlotte Mason's *Parents' Review*, December 1908

My Weekly Schedule in 1996

	M	T	W	TH	F
9:00- 9:20	Math	Math	Math	Math	
9:20- 9:40	Handwriting	Handwriting	Handwriting	Handwriting	
9:40-10:00	History	History	History	History	
10:00-10:50	Read aloud-Literature	Read aloud-Literature	Read aloud-Literature	Read aloud-Literature	
10:50	Drive to college	Drive to college	Drive to college	Drive to college	Drive to college
11:15-12:00	Lunch	Lunch	Lunch	Lunch	Lunch
12:00	Drill	Drill	Drill	Drill	College pick up
12:20-12:40	Science	Science	Science	Science	P.E. Social
12:40-1:00	Simply Grammar	Simply Grammar	Simply Grammar	Simply Grammar	P.E. Social
1:00-1:20	Latin	Music	Art Appr.	Poetry	P.E.
1:20-2:00	Map work read aloud	Children read aloudr	Children read aloud	Children	P.E.

My 1997 Weekly Schedule

	M	T	W	TH	F
9:00- 9:20	Home School Band	Math	Math	Math	Math
9:25- 9:40	Band	Bible	Bible	Bible	Math
9:45- 9:55	Band	Handwriting/Phonics w/1st grdr	Handwriting/Phonics w/1st grdr	Handwriting/Phonics w/1st grdr	Handwriting/Phonics w/1st grdr
10:00- 10:20	Band	History—2 books	Poetry	History—2 books	Spelling test
10:25- 10:40	Band	Dictation	Dictation	Dictation	Dictation
10:45- 11:00	Math	Free Time	Free Time	Free Time	P.E./Social Time
11:05- 11:20	History—2 books	Rote Drill	Rote Drill	Music Appr.	"
11:25- 11:45	Dictation	Science Reading —2 books	Science Reading —2 books	Science Reading —2 books	"
11:50- 12:10	Map work	Greek/Latin	Recitation-Poetry Mem	Art Appr.	"
12:20- 12:40	Lunch	Lunch	Lunch	Lunch	"
12:45- 1:05	Science Reading —2 books	Poetry	Literature—Fiction	Literature—Fiction	"

Continued on next page

	M	T	W	TH	F
1:10- 1:25	Recitation-Poetry	Mem.Spelling (6th grdr.)/ Read aloud-(3rd grdr.)	Written Narrations	Spelling	"
1:30- 1:55	Bible/ Literature	Nature Study/Walk	Nature Study/Walk	Nature Study/Walk	"
2:00- 2:20	Written Narrations (6th grdr.)/ Read aloud-(3rd grdr.)	Free Time	Free Time	Free Time	"
2:20- 3:00	Free Time	"	"	"	"
3:00- 4:30	"	"	"	"	"
4:30- 5:00	Music Practice	Piano Lesson 6th grdr. Spanish (optional)	Music Practice/ 6th grdr. Spanish (optional)	Music Practice/	

My 1998 Weekly Schedule

	M	T	W	TH	F	Sat
8:00 9:00	Listen to Piano Tape	Listen to Piano Tape	Listen to Piano Tape	Listen to Piano Tape	Listen to Piano Tape	Listen to Piano Tape
9:00 10:00	Get ready for BandPractice	PianoPractice	PianoPractice	PianoPractice	PianoPractice	Piano
10:00- 10:20	Band	Math	Math	Math	Math (Younger Children)	
10-20- 10:40	Band	Bible	Bible	Bible	Math (Continues for Older Child)	
10:40- 10:50	Band	Handwriting (Older Children) Phonics with Younger Children	Handwriting (Older Children) Phonics with Younger Children	Handwriting	Phonics	
10:50 11:15	Band	History —2 books	Poetry	History —2 books	Spelling test	
11:20 11:35	Band	Dictation	Dictation	Dictation	Dictation	
11:40 11:50	Band	Free Time	Free Time	Free Time	PE-Social	
11:50 12:05	Math	Rote Drill	Rote Drill	Music	PE-Social	
12:10 12:30	Dictation	Science Reading —2 books	Science Reading —2 books	Science Reading —2 books	PE-Social	

Continued on next page

	M	T	W	TH	F
12:35 12:50	Map work	Greek/Latin	Recitation-Poetry Mem	Art Appr.	PE-Social
1:00 1:30	Lunch	Lunch	Lunch	Lunch	PE-Social
1:35 2:00	History Poetry Mem	Poetry	Literature —Fiction	Literature —Fiction	PE-Social
2:00 2:15	Recitation -Poetry Mem.	Spelling	Written Narrations (older children) read aloud practice for younger children	Spelling	PE-Social
	Literature —Fiction	Bible	Nature Study/ Walk	Nature Study/ Walk	PE-Social
4:30 5:00	Written Narrations (older children) read aloud practice for younger children		Piano Lesson		

General Charlotte Mason Home Schooling Book and Supply List

BOOKS
One well written book on:
- The history of art (prints not necessary)
- The history of music
- Collect various biographies of the poets, composers, scientists, artists, etc.
- One poetry anthology

Collect substantial amounts of:
- Literature
- Poetry
- Art prints and/or coffee table art books
- Field guides (e.g., butterflies, trees, birds, etc.)
- Quality "living books" on various topics (e.g., countries, people, exploration)

Quality reference books on:
- The foreign language you are studying
- Religion (e.g., English, Greek, Hebrew concordances)
- Each branch of science (e.g., astronomy, anatomy etc.)

Other reference materials:
- Dictionary
- Thesaurus
- A set of used Encyclopedias
- Atlas

Curriculum

- Math (there is no C. Mason math text available at this time, you must *adapt* the book to fit your philosophy or use it as designed)
- *Simply Grammar*

Optional curriculum:

- Supplemental workbooks *if you desire* for any subject. (e.g., geography and/or map skills, spelling, handwriting, language arts, foreign lang., high school level science and/ or grammar. Avoid textbooks/workbooks for history whenever possible.)

S<small>UPPLIES</small>
- Sketchbooks
- Paints
- Paint brushes (the best money can buy)
- Field microscope (e.g., Brock Magiscopes)
- Magnifying glass (one for each child)
- Microscope (optional)
- Gardening supplies
- Field coats and boots
- Composition books (for copy work)
- Three ring binders (for narrations, pressed flowers in protective page covers, memorized poems, century books)
- Used musical instruments (save your money for the lessons!)
- Music to play (available at libraries)
- Scrap lumber, nails, screws, paint, tools for free time (check with any carpenter for discards)
- Calculator (for each child)
- Computer (optional)

Recommended Books and Resources

CHARLOTTE MASON'S LIST
The following titles were obtained from Charlotte's own writings. These reflect a large portion of the books used in her schools however, a few were not listed especially if they sounded like standard curriculum such as an arithmetic text or German text. Many of her recommendations will not be easily accessible. Titles designated by an asterisk (*) denote those that I either own or have viewed.—*Catherine*

Literature
Adventures of Beowulf, The
AESOP—*Aesop's Fables* *
ANDERSEN, HANS CHRISTIAN—*Andersen's Fairy Tales*
BOSWELL—*The Battle of the Books*
BULFINCH, THOMAS—*Bulfinch's Age of Fable* *
BUNYAN, JOHN—*Pilgrim's Progress* *
CARLYLE, THOMAS—*Essay on Burns*
CARROLL, LEWIS—*Alice's Adventures in Wonderland* *
DEFOE, DANIEL—*Robinson Crusoe* *
DICKENS, CHARLES—*David Copperfield* *

GOLDSMITH—*Citizen of the World*
GRIMM, THE BROTHERS—*Grimm's Fairy Tales*
HAWTHORNE, NATHANIEL—*Tanglewood Tales*
KEARY—*The Heroes of Asgard*
KINGSLEY, CHARLES—*Water Babies**
KIPLING, RUDYARD—*Just So Stories*
LAMB, CHARLES AND MARY—*Tales From Shakespeare**
LANG, ANDREW—*Tales of Troy and Greece, Little Duke, The*
LONGFELLOW, HENRY WADSWORTH—*The Discoverer of the North Cape; Saga of King Olaf**
MACAULAY—*Essays on Goldsmith*
MALORY—*The Coming of Arthur*
MOORE, FRANKFORT—*Jessamy Bride*
POPE, ALEXANDER—*Essay on Man**
SCOTT, SIR WALTER—*Rob Roy*
SHAKESPEARE, WILLIAM—*Twelfth Night*; Julius Caesar*;* all histories*
She stoops to Conquer (a play)
STEVENSON, ROBERT LOUIS—*Kidnapped**
SWIFT, JONATHAN—*Gulliver's Travels*
THACKERAY, WILLIAM MAKEPEACE—*The Virginians*

FOREIGN LANGUAGES
PARTINGTON, VIOLET—*Siepmann's Primary French Course French Songs*

LANGUAGE ARTS
MASON, CHARLOTTE—*First Grammar Lessons* Now available as
    Simply Grammar* by Karen Andreola.
MEIKLEJOHN—*Short English Grammar*

SCIENCE
BUCKLEY, ARABELLA—*Plant Life in Field and Garden*
BUCKLEY, ARABELLA—*Life and Her Children** (c1880);
    The Fairyland of Science* (c1878)
GATTY, MARGARET SCOTT—*Parables From Nature** (c1855)
HOLDEN, EDWARD SINGLETON—*The Sciences**
JOYCE—*Scientific Dialogues*
BUCKLEY, ARABELLA—*Plant Life in Field and Garden*
KINGSLEY, CHARLES—*Madam How and Lady Why**
Picciola
OLIVER—*Elementary Botany*
DR. SCHOLFIELD—*Physiology for Schools*

SELOUS, EDMUND—*Jack's Insects**
Various authors recomendmended for nature reading: Professor Miall,
    Mrs. Fisher, Mrs. Brightwen, Professor Lloyd Morgan,
    Professor Geikie, Professors Geddes & Thomson

MUSIC
MRS. CURWEN—*Child Pianist*

HISTORY
BEDE—*Ecclesiastical History of England*
CREIGHTON, MRS.—*First History of France* Covers 55 B.C. to A.D. 910.
DEVIZES & deVINSANY—*Chronicles of the Crusades*
FORSTER, ARNOLD—*A History Of England** Covers 55 B.C. to A.D. 910.
GEOFFREY—*History of the British Kings*
GREEN—*Shorter History of England*
HUNT, BROOKE—*Prisoners of the Tower*
KINGSLEY, CHARLES—*Alton Locke; Westward Ho*
LORD—*Modern Europe*
LORD, MRS. FREWEN—*Tales from St. Paul's; Tales from Westminster Abbey**
PLUTARCH—*Lives**
POWELL, YORK—*Old Stories from British History; Sketches from British History*
SCOTT, SIR WALTER—*Waverly*
SCOTT, SIR WALTER—*Quentin Druward; The Talisman*

GEOGRAPHY
GEIKIE —*Physical Geography*
HOUSEHOLD, H. W.—*Our Sea Power**
MASON, CHARLOTTE—*The Ambleside Geography Books*
PARKIN, SIR GEORGE—*Round the Empire*

CITIZENSHIP
BEESLEY, MRS.—*Stories from the History of Rome*
FORSTER, ARNOLD—*A Citizen Reader*
PLUTARCH—*Julius Caesar**

BIBLE
AGE 6 TO 8: Read to them both OT and NT, concentrating on the
Gospels and Acts.
BY 9: Read to themselves simple OT passages and two of the Gospels.
BY 12: They have covered all the OT and have concentrated on the
Epistles and Revelation.
AGE 12 TO 15: Read to themselves all the OT.

AGE 15 TO 18: Read commentaries.
Additional Bible Related Reading
DR. ABBOT—*Bible Lessons*
Northumbrian Saints, The
Sidelights on the Bible
Wigwam Stories

Catherine Levison's List

The following is a list of books that I own and can recommend, either because I have read a book in its entirety or have read enough of it to purchase it for our homeschool. This list does not include the many educational, hands-on items that are also necessary (and fun) for developing an atmosphere of education in the home or classroom. —*Catherine*

LITERATURE
ALCOTT, LOUISA MAY—*Eight Cousins; Jo's Boys; Little Men; Little Women*
AUSTEN, JANE—*Emma; Persuasion; Pride and Prejudice; Sense & Sensibility*
BLOS, JOAN W.—*A Gathering of Days*
BRONTË, CHARLOTTE—*Jane Eyre*
BRONTË, EMILY—*Wuthering Heights*
BURNETT, FRANCES H.—*A Little Princess; The Secret Garden*
CHAUNDLER, CHRISTINE—*Lancelot*
Complete Mother Goose, The
DICKENS, CHARLES—*A Tale of Two Cities; Bleak House; Oliver Twist*
DODGE, MARY MAPES—*Hans Brinker or The Silver Skates*
ELIOT, GEORGE—*Brother Jacob; Middlemarch; Silas Marner; The Lifted Veil*
FORSTER, E. M.—*A Room With a View; Howards End;*
    Where Angels Fear to Tread
HAWTHORNE, NATHANIEL—*The House of Seven Gables;*
    The Scarlet Letter; Twice Told Tales
JAMES, HENRY—*The Portrait of a Lady; The Turn of the Screw*
KIPLING, RUDYARD—*The Jungle Book*
LONDON, JACK—*The Call of the Wild*
MACDONALD, GEORGE—*At the Back of the North Wind*
MARSHALL, H. E.—*English Literature* (c1909)
MILNE, A. A.—*The House at Pooh Corner; Winnie-the-Pooh*
MONTGOMERY, L. M.—*Anne of Green Gables; Anne of Avonlea*
PASTERNAK, BORIS—*Dr. Zhivago*
PORTER, ELEANOR H.—*Pollyana*
POTTER, BEATRIX—*The Complete Tales of Beatrix Potter*

RHEAD, LOUISE—*Robin Hood*
SEWELL, ANNA—*Black Beauty*
SPYRI, JOHANNA—*Heidi*
ST. JOHN, PATRICIA—*Treasures of the Snow*
STEVENSON, ROBERT LOUIS—*Treasure Island*
TERHUNE, ALBERT—*Great Dog Stories*
THOMAS, DYLAN—*Quite Early One Morning*
THOREAU, HENRY DAVID—*Walden*
TWAIN, MARK—*The Prince and the Pauper*
VERNON, LOUISE—*Key to the Prison*
WARTON, EDITH—*The Custom of the Country*
WATSON, VIRGINIA—*The Legend of Pocahontas*
WIGGIN, KATE DOUGLAS—*Rebecca of Sunnybrook Farm*
WILDER, LAURA INGALLS—*Little House* series
WOUK, HERMAN—*The Caine Mutiny*
WYSS, JOHANN—*The Swiss Family Robinson*

POETRY

ARMSTRONG & BRISTOW—*Nineteenth-Century Women Poets*
BROWNING, ELIZABETH BARRETT—*Selected Poems*
BROWNING, ROBERT—*Browning's Complete Poetical Works*
BURROUGHS, JOHN—*Bird and Bough*
BYRON, LORD GEORGE—*Childe Harold*
FERRIS, HELEN—*Favorite Poems Old and New*
FROST, ROBERT—*Robert Frost Selected Poems*
GARDNER, MARTIN—*Best Remembered Poems*
PAGE, CURTIS H.—*The Chief American Poets* (c1905)
SCOTT, SIR WALTER—*Lady of the Lake*
STEVENSON, ROBERT LOUIS—*A Child's Garden of Verses*
WINGS BOOKS—*The Book of 1000 Poems*

FOREIGN LANGUAGES

Greek:
BERRY, GEORGE RICKER—*Interlinear Greek-English New Testament* ZODHIATES—*The Complete Word Study New Testament*

Greek and Hebrew:
GREEN, JAY P.—*The Interlinear Bible* (4 vol.)

Greek and Latin:
LUNDQUIST—*English From the Roots Up*
Flashcards. *Rummy Roots*

Spanish:
CROWN PUBLISHERS—*Children's Living Spanish* Tape and book (Recommended: Tape only).

Latin:
LONGMAN—*Ecce Romani* 1A and 1B with the activity sheets and teacher guides. The ordering numbers are: 79741 teacher guide, 79728 1A student's book, 79729 1B student's book, 79733 activity workbook, and 79734 activity workbook.

LANGUAGE ARTS
ANDREOLA, KAREN—*Simply Grammar*
STOUT, KATHRYIN—*Natural Speller*
The ABC's and All Their Tricks

SCIENCE
BURROUGHS, JOHN—*Squirrels and Other Fur Bearers* (c1875)
CHRISTIAN LIBERTY PRESS—*Nature Readers*
COMSTOCK, ANNA—*Handbook of Nature Study*
DARLING, LOUIS—*Greenhead* A story about ducks.
DORROS, ARTHUR—*A Tree is Growing* For grade school.
HOLDEN, EDITH—*The Country Diary of an Edwardian Lady*
HORNBLOW—*Birds Do the Strangest Things*
KATZ, ADRIENNE—*Naturewatch; Exploring Nature with Your Children*
LESLIE & ROTH—*Nature Journaling* (non Christian)
LOVEJOY, SHARON—*Hollyhock Days; Garden Adventures for the Young at Heart*
LOVEJOY, SHARON—*Sunflower Houses; Garden Discoveries for Children of All Ages*
RHOADES, DIANE—*Garden Crafts for Kids*
SETON, ERNEST THOMPSON—*Wild Animals I Have Known*
STODDART, JULIA—*Strange Birds at the Zoo* (c1929)
TUNIS, EDWIN—*Chipmunks on the Doorstep* (c1971)
WICK, WALTER—*A Drop of Water* A picture book.

MATH
HANSEN, JAYE—*Grocery Cart Math*
MCCABE, JOHN L. P.—*Applying Algebra* (Publisher: Garlic Press)
REIMER, LUETTA AND WILBERT—*Mathematicians Are People, Too; Stories From the Lives of Great Mathematicians*

MUSIC
BAUER, MARION AND ETHEL PEYSER—*How Music Grew* (c1925)

GARDNER, PENNY—*Nine-Note Recorder Method; Easy Duets for Beginners*
KAVANAUGH, PATRICK—*Music of the Great Composers; The Spiritual Lives of the Great Composers*

EDUCATION—*Also see Further Study Chapter*
GARDNER, PENNY—*Charlotte Mason Study Guide*
MACAULAY, SUSAN SCHAEFFER—*For the Children's Sake*
MASON, CHARLOTTE—*Home Education Series* (6 vol.)
RUSHTON, CINDY—Language Arts . . .The Easy Way
WILSON, CALLIHAN & JONES - *Classical Education & The Home School*

MISCELLANEOUS
ARNOLD, ELEANOR—*Voices of American Homemakers* (c1985)
BAN BREATHNACH, SARAH—*Victorian Family Celebrations* (also known as *Mrs. Sharp's Traditions*)
BEARD, DANIEL—*The American Boys Handy Book*
BEARD, LINA AND ADELIA—*The American Girls Handy Book*
DISCHE & ENZENSBERGER—*Esterhazy* For younger children.
KALMAN, BOBBIE—*Food for the Settler; Home Crafts* For younger children.
LOCKER, THOMAS—*The Boy Who Held Back the Sea; Where the River Begins* For younger children.
TRUMBULL, CLAY—*Hints on Child Training*
TUDOR, BETHANY—*Drawn From New England*
WILSON, LAURA—*Daily Life in a Victorian House* For younger children.

HISTORY
ANTHONY, KATHARINE—*Queen Elizabeth* (c1929)
Apology, Phaedo and Crito of Plato, The
BOWEN, CATHERINE—*John Adams and the American Revolution* (c1949)
BRENNER, BARBARA—*If You Were There in 1776* For grade school.
BULFINCH—*Bulfinch's Mythology*
BUREAU OF NATIONAL LITERATURE INC. - *Messages and Papers of the Presidents* (Vol. 15)
CARLYLE, THOMAS—*The French Revolution*
CASKODEN, EDWIN—*When Knighthood was in Flower* (c1898)
CHRISTIAN LIBERTY PRESS—*Stories of the Pilgrims; History Stories for Children*
DICKENS, CHARLES—*A Child's History of England*
FRANKLIN, BENJAMIN—*The Autobiography and Other Writings*
LORD MACAULAY—*History of England* (Four Volumes)
    Golden Sayings of Epictetus, The

GRUN, BERNARD—*The Timetables of History*
HATCHER, CAROLYN—*Let the Authors Speak* A book list.
HENTY, G. A.—*In Freedom's Cause*
HOLT, RACKHAM—*George Washington Carver* (c1943)
HUBERT—*Men of Achievement*
HUNT, JOHN G—*Words of Our Nation* (c1993)
KALMAN, BOBBIE—*Early Christmas*
KELLER, HELEN—*The Story of My Life*
KETCHUM, LISA—*The Gold Rush*
Kingfisher Illustrated History of the World, The A reference book similar to Dorling/
  Kindersley books.
LOCKLEY, FRED—*Conversations with Pioneer Women*
LOCKHART, J. G.—*Memoirs of Sir Walter Scott*
LOEPER, JOHN J.—*Going to School in 1776*
MACGREGOR, MARY—*The Story of Greece* (c1959); *The Story of Rome* (c1959)
MARSHALL, H. E.—*Our Island Story; Our Empire Story; Scotland's Story*
MCMASTER, JOHN BACH—*Brief History of the United States* (c1907)
Meditations of Marcus Aurelius, The
MEEKER, EZRA—*The Tragedy of Leschi; Uncle Ezra's Short Stories for Children,*
  Seventy Years of Progress in Washington [State]
MONTGOMERY, WALTER—*Stories of the French Revolution* (c1893)
POOL, DANIEL—*What Jane Austen Ate and Charles Dickens Knew*
PRATT, MARA—*American History Stories... You Never Read in School...but should*
  have
ROOKIE BIOGRAPHY—*Albert Schweitzer; Elizabeth the First; Christopher Columbus*
  Good readers for younger children.
SCHLISSEL, LILLIAN—*Women's Diaries of the Westward Journey*
SCHMIDT, GORG AND HANS—*Ludwig Van Beethoven* (c1970)
SCHOLASTIC—*If You Grew Up With Abraham Lincoln; If You Grew Up With George*
  Washington; If You Sailed on the Mayflower Good readers for younger children.
STANLEY, DIANE AND PETER VENNEMA—*Bard of Avon*
TAPPAN, EVE MARCH—*England's Story* (A living textbook)
WHIPPLE, WAYNE—*Abraham Lincoln's Don'ts* (c1918)
WHITE, TRUMELL—*Our New Possessions* (c1898) About the Philippines, Cuba,
  Puerto Rico, and Hawaii.

Geography
PRESBYTER IGNOTUS—*Travel Pictures* (c1912)
STORY BEHIND THE SCENERY—*Oregon Trail; Lewis and Clark; North Cascades;*
  The Santa Fe Trail These are mainly pictorial.

Art
CRAVEN, THOMAS—*Men of Art* (c1931) A history of art; no prints.

Collect prints from museums, frame stores, and antique shops; collect catalogs from museums and print stores; and obtain art books from the library. Calendars are another excellent source.

I've collected a lot of art prints, but I would like to recommend two easy-to-obtain, currently available resources: *American Artists Reflect American History* (vol. 1–4) Five huge prints per volume. SIMON AND SCHUSTER (publisher)—*Stories From the New Testament* Includes 17 well-chosen paintings.

OTHER CHARLOTTE MASON PARENTS' LIST

This list was gathered by asking C. Mason home schoolers from around the world to recommend the best living book that they had ever *used* in their homeschools and classrooms. Although I've read some of them, I have not read them all. —*Catherine*

ALLEN, DOUGLAS AND DOUGLAS ALLEN, JR.—*N. C. Wyeth* (c1972, reprinted 1996 by Wing Books, pp 192) An art book.
AMBROSE, STEPHEN E.—*Undaunted Courage* (ISBN 0-684-82697-6) The biography of Meriwether Lewis.
ANDERSON, MARGARET—*Children of Summer*
BARKER, CICELY MARY—*Flower Fairies*
BEECHICK, RUTH—*Adam and His Kin* (ISBN 0-940319-07-1)
BENDICK, JOANNE—*Archimedes and the Door of Science*
BJORK, CHRISTINA, LENA ANDERSON—*Linnea in Monet's Garden* (ISBN 91-29-58314-1)
BRINK, CAROL RYRIE—*Caddie Woodlawn*
BROOKHISER, RICHARD (editor)—*Rules of Civility: The 110 Precepts That Guided Our First President in War and Peace* (c1997, pp 88) For moral training.
BUNYAN, JOHN—*Dangerous Journey*
BURGESS, THORNTON—*The Burgess Bird Book for Children* (c1919)
CANFIELD, DOROTHY—*Understood Betsy*
CARAS, ROGER—A natural history author.
Childhood of Famous Americans series
CHURCHILL, WINSTON (see Commager)—*The History of the English-Speaking People* (4-vol. set)
COMMAGER, HENRY STEELE (see Churchill)—*The History of the English-Speaking People* (edited and arranged to one volume)
COOK, ROY J., editor—*One Hundred and One Famous Poems* (c1958, pp 193) For high school.
D'AULAIRE, INGRI AND EDGAR PARIN—All history books

DALGLIESH, ALICE—*The Courage of Sarah Noble*

DAUGHERTY, JAMES—*Landing of the Pilgrims, The* (Landmark series) (c1950, pp 151)

DE JONG, MEINDERT—*The Wheel on the School* (ISBN 0-06-440021-2)

FABRE, JEAN HENRI—*Insects*

FARJEAN, ELEANOR—*Mighty Men* (c1925) Available through Calvert.

FORBES, ESTHER—*Johnny Tremain; Paul Revere and the World He Lived In* (c1942, pp 478)

FOSTER, GENEVIEVE—*The World of Augustus Caesar; The World of Columbus and Sons*

GEORGE, JEAN CRAIGHEAD—*My Side of the Mountain*

GIBBONS, GAIL—*Knights in Shining Armor*

GRANT, GEORGE—*Patriot's Handbook, The* (c1996, pp 464) For high school.

HAMMOND, SUSAN—*Beethoven Lives Upstairs*

HAWTHORNE, NATHANIEL—*Wonder Book*

HAYS, WILMA PITCHFORD—*Eli Whitney: Founder of Modern Industry* (Immortals of Engineering series) (c1965, pp 91)

HENRY, MARGUERITE—*Benjamin West and His Cat Grimalkin; Robert Fulton, Boy Craftsman*

HENRY, RALPH AND LUCILLE PANNELL—*My American Heritage* (Publisher: Rand McNally)

HERRIOT, JAMES—*Treasury for Children*

JUDSON, PHOEBE GOODELL — *A Pioneer's Search for an Ideal Home*

RAWICZ, SLAVOMIR — *The Long Walk*

HILLYER, V. M.—*A Child's History of the World* (Available from M. F. Alder, Box 627, Stockbridge, MA 01262, 413-298-3559); *A Child's Geography of the World*

HOLLING, HOLLING CLANCY—*Paddle-to-the-*Sea (c1941, renewed 1969, pp 27); *Pagoo* (ISBN 0-395-53964-1)

HOSKIN, MICHAEL, editor—*Astronomy, The Cambridge Illustrated History of* (c1997, pp 392) Great reference book for high school.

HUBBARD, ELBERT—*Little Journeys to the Homes of Emminent Painters* (c1899, pp 497 short pages) Lengthy narratives of 12 artists.

HUTCHINSON, FREDERICK WINTHROP—*The Men Who Found America* (c1909; Publisher: Edward Stern & Co. Inc.)

KERR, JOAN PETERSON, editor—*A Bully Father: Theodore Roosevelt's Letters to His Children* (c1995, pp 248)

LATTIMORE, ELEANOR—*Little Pear*

LEA, ROSEMARY—*Miss Lea's Bible Stories for Children*

LENSKI, LOIS—*Houseboat Girl* (c1957); *Indian Captive; Strawberry Girl; Prairie School*

LEVI, PETER—*The Life and Time of William Shakespeare* (c1988; ISBN 0-517-14698-3)

LEWIS, C. S.—*Chronicles of Narnia*

LITTLESUGAR, AMY—*Marie in Fourth Position: The Story of Degas' "The Little Dancer"*

MACDONALD, GEORGE—All books.

MACLACHLAN, PATRICIA AND MIKE WIMMER—*All the Place to Love* (ISBN 0-06-021098 -2)

MCCLOSKEY, ROBERT—*One Morning in Maine* (ISBN 0-670-53627-4)

MCGRAW, ELOISE, J.—*The Golden Goblet; Mara, Daughter of the Nile* Recreational reading aloud in order to omit some passages.

MCHUGH, MICHAEL J. AND DR. CHARLES MORRIS—*A Child's Story of America* (c1989, Christian Liberty Press, pp 279) A very good overview for fourth graders. Can intersperse with living books for a more thorough study.

MEADOWCROFT, WILLIAM—*The Boys' Life of Edison* (Boys' Life series) (c1911, pp 272)

MILLER, FRANCIS TREVELYAN—*Hero Tales from American Life* (c1909, pp 454) 100 short, true stories of courageous men, women, and children. For moral training.

MONTGOMERY, RUTHERFORD—A natural history author.

MOODY, RALPH—*The Little Britches* series

MORRISON, LUCILE—*The Lost Queen of Egypt* (c1937; Publisher: J. B. Lippincott Co., LCCC: 37-28730)

MOWAT, FARLEY—*Owls in the Family*

MURPHY, ROBERT—A natural history author.

OPTIC, OLIVER—*Rich and Humble* and all other books. Check availability with Mantle Ministries.

ORCZY, BARONESS—*Scarlet Pimpernel, The* (c1905, republished 1997 by Puffin Books, pp 323)

PETRY, ANN—*Harriet Tubman, Conductor of the Underground Railroad*

PORTER, GENE STRATTON—*The Girl of the Limberlost*

PRICE, L. AND LEWIS CHRISMAN—*Selections from Lincoln* (c1912; Publisher: D. C. Heath & Co.)

PUMPHREY, MARGARET B.—*Stories of the Pilgrims*

RAWLINGS, MARJORIE KINNAN—*The Yearling*

RAWLS, WILSON—*Where the Red Fern Grows*

SCARF, MAGGIE—*Antarctica: Exploring the Frozen Continent* (c1970)

SCHAEFFER, FRANCIS—*How Should We Then Live?* (c1976, pp 265) Great overview of Christian worldview perspectives for high schoolers.

SCHLIEN, MIRIAM—*Lucky Porcupine*

SCOTT, FORESMAN & CO.—*Science Stories*

SETON, ERNEST THOMPSON—(A natural history author)

SHUTTLESWORTH, DOROTHY—*Exploring Nature with Your Child*

SPEARE, ELIZABETH GEORGE—*The Bronze Bow; The Sign of the Beaver*

SPURGEON, CHARLES HADDON—*A Good Start: A Book for Young Men and Women* (c1898, reprinted 1995 by Soli Deo Gloria, pp 329) For moral training.

ST. JOHN, PATRICIA—All books.

STANLEY, DIANE—*The Librarian Who Measured the Earth* About early Greek scientist, Eratosthenes.

STEPHENS, C. A.—*Stories From the Old Squire's Farm* (c1995, compiled and edited by Charles G. and Eric-Jon Waugh, pp 408) Written in the 1800s.

STEVENSON, O. J.—*Talking Wire: The Story of Alexander Graham Bell* (c1947, pp 201)

STRONG, JAY—*Heroic Stories of Famous Men and Women* (c1955)

THAYER, WILLIAM M.—*From Log Cabin to the White House: Life of James A. Garfield* (c1883, pp 483)

VAN LOON, HENDRIK—*Story of Mankind*

VOS, CATHERINE F.—*The Child's Story Bible* (ISBN 0-8028-5011-1)

WINNICK—*Mr. Lincoln's Whiskers*

Book Lists Books

HATCHER, CAROLYN — *Let the Authors Speak*

LET'S HEAR IT FOR THE GIRLS—A list of books for girls aged four to fourteen.

MILLER, CHRISTINE — *All Through the Ages*

ROBERTS, HELEN — *Buried Treasure*

WILSON, ELIZABETH — *Books Children Love*

Charlotte Mason Parents' Resources
Where to Find Books

Many parents have suggested library sales for acquiring books, where they sell their discards. I agree—some of the best books I own have "Discarded" stamped on them. Also mentioned were garage sales, antique shops and used bookstores. Going through relatives' storage areas was another good tip. And don't forget those interlibrary loans!
—*Catherine*

BOOK-SEARCH SERVICES
ABRACADABRA (ANTIQUARIAN) BOOKSHOP & BOOKSEARCH INTERNA-
TIONAL—32 South Broadway, Denver, Colorado 80209-1506, 800-545-
2665, FAX 303-871-0172, e-mail: abrabks@abrabks.com
INTERNET: abebooks.com; bibliofind.com; mxbf.com; barnesandnoble.com;
amazon.com
RED BRIDGE BOOKS—2523 Red Bridge Terrace, Kansas City, Missouri 64131,
816-942-0106. Free out-of-print book search service.
BARGAIN TABLES at new bookstores.
BARNES & NOBLE

OTHER SOURCES
BEAUTIFUL FEET catalog
BETHLEHEM BOOKS—PO Box 2338, Ft. Collins, CO 80522, 800-757-6831.
Reprints of children's books.
CONSERVATIVE BOOK CLUB—One Massachusetts Avenue, N.W. Suite 600,
Washington, D.C. or PO Box 97197 Washington, D.C. 20090-7197
CROWN BOOKS SUPERSTORES
DAD'S OLD BOOKS in Nashville, TN
DOVER PUBLICATIONS catalog—31 E. 2nd St., Mineola, NY 11501
ELIJAH COMPANY catalog—1053 Eldridge Loop, Crossville, TN 38558, 888-2-
ELIJAH, www.elijahco.com
GREENLEAF PRESS catalog—3761 Hwy 109N, Unit D, Lebanon, TN 37087,
615-449-1617, www.greenleafpress.com
HALF-PRICE BOOKS
HALLMARK STORES have *Nature's Sketchbook* by Marjolein Bastin. The words and
beautifully detailed pictures are so inspiring.
LIBRARY—Annual sale.
LIFETIME BOOKS & GIFTS catalog—3900 Chalet Suzanne Drive, Lake Wales, FL
33853-7763, 800-377-0390 (order phone *only* please),
www.lifetimeonline.com
SMITH'S FAMILY BOOKSTORES in Eugene, Oregon
SONLIGHT CURRICULUM BOOKS catalog—8121 South Grant Way, Littleton,
CO 80122-2701, 303-730-6292, www.sonlight.com

WHERE TO FIND ART
ART EXTENSION PRESS—Box 389, Westport, CN 06881
CALENDARS—One Charlotte Mason parent matted the 12 prints on high-quality
card stock for viewing. She and her children take turns pretending they've
never seen the print, while another describes the print in detail. She also used

the 12 small pictures from the back of the calendar to play matching games.

NATIONAL GALLERY OF ART in Washington, D.C.—Available prints can only be viewed through the internet at www.nga.org. Besides prints, the museum shop sells sets by Taschen, which include six prints of one artist in a folder that also has a short biography of the artist.

PRINT DETECTORS—86 Great Oak Lane, Pleasantville, NY 10570, 914-741-2641. This is a retail mail order art gallery specializing in locating and selling prints and posters, many of which are difficult to find. There is no charge for this service.

Bibliography

Avery, D. *Cultural Value of Science*. London, England. Parents' National Educational Union. *The Parents' Review*, September, 1920. Reprinted in *The Skylark*, Fall, 1996

B. H. *History: The Teaching of History*. London, England. Parents' National Educational Union. *The Parents' Review*, November, 1893.

B. H. *History: Teaching Practically Considered*. London, England. Parents' National Educational Union. *The Parents' Review*, December, 1893.

B. H. *History: Teaching Practically Considered No. III*. London, England. Parents' National Educational Union. *The Parents' Review*, January, 1894.

B. H. *History: History and Fiction*. London, England. Parents' National Educational Union. *The Parents' Review*, April, 1894.

Beale, Dorothea, *Psychological Order of Teaching with Special Reference to Natural Science*. London, England. Parents' National Educational Union. *The Parents' Review*, March, 1898.

Beechick, Ruth, Dr. *How Should Homeschoolers Prepare Their Children to Get into College?* Birmingham, AL. *Homeschooling Today*, September/October 1998

Begley, Sharon. *Your Child's Brain*. U.S.A. *Newsweek*. Ferbruary 19, 1996.

Bernau, G. M. *The Book of Centuries and How to Keep One*. London, England. Parents' National Educational Union. *The Parents' Review*. Reprinted: United States, Andreola, Karen. *Parents' Review*, Volume II. Fall, 1992.

Boole, Mary Everest. *Home Arithmetic*. London, England. Parents' National Educational Union. *The Parents' Review*, September, 1893.

Boole, Mary Everest. *Home Algebra and Geometry*. London, England. Parents' National Educational Union. *The Parents' Review*, November, 1893.

Boorstin, Daniel J. *I Cannot Live Without Books*. U.S.A. *Pararde Magazine*. July 12, 1998

Breckels, Eleanor. *Life in a PNEU Nursery School*. 1969

Cholmondeley, Essex. *The Personality of the Teacher*. London, England. Parents' National Education Union. *The Parents' Review*, November, 1919. Reprinted in *The Skylark*, Fall, 1997.

Cholmondeley, Essex. *The Story of Charlotte Mason*. London, England. J. M. Dent & Sons Ltd., 1960.

Claxton, K. M. *Conference Lessons, Class II*. London, England. Parents' National Education Union. *The Parents' Review*, August, 1915. Reprinted in *The Skylark*, Fall, 1997.

Cochrane, Jean, C. *Some Aspects of our work in the Parents' Union School.* London, England. Parents' National Education Union. *The Parents' Review*, October, 1963. Reprinted in *The Skylark*, Spring, 1997.

Cochrane, Jean, C. *Knowledge of Man.* London, England. Parents' National Education Union. *The Parents' Review*, November, 1964. Reprinted in *The Skylark*, Spring, 1997.

Costner, Herbert. *New Perspectives on Liberal Education.* Seattle, Washington. University of Washington Press. 1989

Davies, G. L. *Knowledge of the Universe.* London, England. Parents' National Education Union. *The Parents' Review*, December, 1964. Reprinted in *The Skylark*, Spring, 1997.

DeGaetano, Gloria M. Ed. *Building Stong Minds and Making Wise Media Choices.* U.S.A. *Washington Citizen.* August, 1996

Encyclopedia Americana. #17, 1998.

Encyclopedia Britannica #7, 1998.

Franklin, Henrietta. *The Home Training of Children.* London, England. Parents' National Educational Union. *The Parents' Review*, December, 1908.

Franklin, Henrietta. *The Home Training of Children cont..* London, England. Parents' National Educational Union. *The Parents' Review*, January, 1909.

Frost, Eleanor, M. *Impressions of a Conference Work with Class II.* London, England. Parents' National Education Union. *The Parents' Review*, August, 1915. Reprinted in *The Skylark*, Fall, 1997.

Gibbon, Monk. *Netta.* London, England. Routledge and Kegan Paul Ltd. 1960

Glover, Cedric Howard. *The Term's Music.* London, England. Kegan Paul, Trench, Trubner, & Co., Ltd. 1925

Hardcastle, Mary. *It All Comes Down to Education.* London, England. Parents' National Education Union. *The Parents' Review*, July/August, 1942. Reprinted in *The Skylark*, Fall, 1997.

Husband, G. F. *Some Notes on Narration.* London, England. Parents' National Education Union. *The Parents' Review*, September, 1924. Reprinted in *The Skylark*, Fall, 1997.

Hutchins, Robert Maynard. *The Great Conversation: Volume One of Great Books of the Western World.* U.S.A. William Bent Publishing. 1951

In Memoriam of Charlotte M. Mason. London, England. Parents' National Educational Union. 1923.

Inman, J. P. *Charlotte Mason College.* England. The Cormorant Press. 1985

Keith, Diane Flynn. *Homeschooling Schizophrenia.* Los Angeles, California. *The Link—A Homeschool Newspaper*, Vol. Two, Issue Four

King, Jenny. *Charlotte Mason Reviewed.* Devon, England. Arthur H. Stockwell Ltd. 1981.

Kitching, Elsie. *Concerning "Repeated Narration."* London, England. Parents' National Education Union. *The Parents' Review*, January, 1928. Reprinted in *The Skylark*, Fall, 1997.

Lindsay, Barbara. *Beginning the Adventure of Learning.* London, England. Parents' National Educational Union. *The Parents' Review*. March, 1965.

Manders, E. K. *We Narrate and Then We Know.* London, England. Parents' National Education Union. *The Parents' Review*, July, 1967. Reprinted in *The Skylark*, Fall, 1997.

Mason, Charlotte Marie Shaw. *Home Education*: Volume One of The Home Education Series. London, England: Kegan Paul, Trench, Trubner and Co., Ltd., 1935. Reprinted, Wheaton, Illinois: Tyndale House Publishers, Inc., 1989.

Mason, Charlotte Marie Shaw. *Parents and Children*: Volume Two of The Home Education Series. London, England: Kegan Paul, Trench, Trubner and Co., Ltd., 1904. Reprinted,

Wheaton, Illinois: Tyndale House Publishers, Inc., 1989.

Mason, Charlotte Marie Shaw. *School Education*: Volume Three of The Home Education Series. London, England: Kegan Paul, Trench, Trubner and Co., Ltd., 1907. Reprinted, Wheaton, Illinois: Tyndale House Publishers, Inc., 1989.

Mason, Charlotte Marie Shaw. *Ourselves*: Volume Four of The Home Education Series. London, England: Kegan Paul, Trench, Trubner and Co., Ltd., 1905. Reprinted, Wheaton, Illinois: Tyndale House Publishers, Inc., 1989.

Mason, Charlotte Marie Shaw. *Formation of Character*: Volume Five of The Home Education Series. London, England: Kegan Paul, Trench, Trubner and Co., Ltd., 1906. Reprinted, Wheaton, Illinois: Tyndale House Publishers, Inc., 1989.

Mason, Charlotte Marie Shaw. *A Philosophy of Education*: Volume Six of The Home Education Series. London, England: Kegan Paul, Trench, Trubner and Co., Ltd., 1925. Reprinted, Wheaton, Illinois: Tyndale House Publishers, Inc., 1989.

Mason, Charlotte Marie Shaw. *The Home School*. London, England. Parents' National Educational Union. *The Parents' Review*, April, 1892.

Mason, Charlotte Marie Shaw. *A Liberal Education for All: Parents' Union School Prospectus, Specimen Programmes, suggestions, &c.* London, England. Parents' National Educational Union. (c 1920).

McGechan, Joyce. *To Prosper in Good Life and Good Literature*. London, England. Parents' National Education Union. *The Parents' Review*, January 1967. Reprinted in *The Skylark*, Spring, 1997.

Molyneux, E. L. *Teaching Time*. London, England. Parents' National Educational Union. *The Parents' Review*, February, 1966.

Nadler, Burton Jay. *Liberal Arts Power! What It Is and How to Sell It on Your Resume*. Princeton, New Jersey. Peterson. 1989

O'Ferrall. *The Work and Aims of the Parents' Union School*. London, England. Parents' National Education Union. *The Parents' Review*, November, 1922. Reprinted in *The Skylark*, Spring, 1997.

P. M. *Imaginations as Cultivated by the Teaching of Geography and History*. London, England. Parents' National Educational Union. *The Parents' Review*, February, 1895.

PNEU School: Independent Day School. London, England. World Wide Education Service of the PNEU. May, 1987

Pennethorne, R. A... PNEU *Principles as Illustrated by Teaching*. London, England. Parents' National Educational Union. *The Parents' Review*, September, 1899.

Seeley, Rev. Henry. *How to Teach the Bible to our Children*. London, England. Parents' National Educational Union. *The Parents' Review*, January, 1895.

Seeley, Rev. Henry. *How to Teach the Bible to our Children, No. II*. London, England. Parents' National Educational Union. *The Parents' Review*, February, 1895.

Seeley, Rev. Henry. *How to Teach the Bible to our Children, No. III*. London, England. Parents' National Educational Union. *The Parents' Review*, March, 1895.

Seeley, Rev. Henry. *How to Teach the Bible to our Children, No. IV*. London, England. Parents' National Educational Union. *The Parents' Review*, April, 1895.

Webb, Helen, Dr. *Children and the Stress of Life*. London, England. Parents' National Educational Union. 1929.

Webster's Collegiate Dictionary Tenth Edition. U.S.A. Merriam-Webster, Inc. 1993

Wilson, Douglas. Callihan, Wesley. Jones, Douglas. *Classical Education & The Home School* Moscow, Idaho. Canon Press. 1995

Wix, H. E. *The PNEU Method in Sunday Schools*. London, England. Parents' National Educational Union. *The Parents' Review*, November, 1917. Reprinted in *The Skylark*, Fall 1996

Wix, H. E. *The PNEU in Sunday Schools, No. II*. London, England. Parents' National Educational Union. *The Parents' Review*, April, 1918.

Wix, Helen, E. *Some Thoughts on Narration*. London, England. Parents' National Education Union. *The Parents' Review*, February, 1957. Reprinted in *The Skylark*, Fall, 1997.

World Book Encyclopedia, the. #12, 1976.

World Book Encyclopedia, the. #6, 1976

A Charlotte Mason EDUCATION

BY CATHERINE LEVISON $8.95
ISBN 1-891400-16-9

The immensely popular ideas of Charlotte Mason have inspired educators for many decades. Her unique methodology as written about in her six-volume series established the necessary protocols for an education above and beyond that which can be found in traditional classroom settings. In *A Charlotte Mason Education*, Catherine Levison has collected the key points of Charlotte Mason's methods and presents them in a simple, straightforward way that will allow families to quickly maximize the opportunities of homeschooling. With weekly schedules, a challenging and diverse curriculum will both inspire and educate your child. *A Charlotte Mason Education* is the latest tool for parents seeking the best education for their children.

More Charlotte Mason EDUCATION

BY CATHERINE LEVISON $13.95
ISBN   1-891400-17-7

Thousands of home educators benefited from the practical ideas contained Catherine Levison's primer, *A Charlotte Mason Education*. Now Catherine takes an in-depth journey offering even more ideas for implementing the popular methods of Charlotte Mason into home schooling. In this concise and practical guide, Levison presents the key points of Charlotte Mason's methods as contained in her six-volume series. A perfect companion to her first book, *More Charlotte Mason Education* will continue to guide your family down an enjoyable and successful path of home schooling.

BACK TO BASICS:
101 Ideas for Strengthening Our Children and Our Families

BY BROOK NOEL $13.95
ISBN   1-891400-48-7

"Life is what happens while we're making other plans," the adage goes, but how far have modern families let that attitude take root? Too far, it would seem, when a recent survey found that the average working mother spends 50 minutes a day with her child. The average working father? Nine! It doesn't have to be. In her new book, author Brook Noel confronts the issues that continue to tear at the modern social fabric. Noel's collection of insights offer a much-needed road map back to the values that are the foundation for strong homes and strong families.

FROZEN ASSETS:
HOW TO COOK FOR A DAY AND EAT FOR A MONTH

BY DEBORAH TAYLOR-HOUGH $14.95
ISBN   1-891400-61-4

Frozen Assets offers a step-by-step plan for spending less time in the kitchen without sacrificing nutrition value. By using these methods one can spend just one day in the kitchen each month and still enjoy a homemade meal for breakfast, lunch and dinner—every day of the month! The book contains a complete outline for those looking to benefit from this cooking revolution. With a two-week plan a one-month plan and a ten-day plan to avoid cooking over the holidays, this book is the answer to the prayers of many families seeking remedies that save time and money. Complete with shopping lists, low-fat tips, ideas for singles, instruction for adapting your own recipes and freezing guidelines, the book is the one-stop resource for those looking to increase their time at the family table and decrease their time in the kitchen and drive-through lanes.

365 QUICK, EASY AND INEXPENSIVE DINNER MENUS

BY PENNY E. STONE $18.95
ISBN   1-891400-33-9

365 Quick, Easy and Inexpensive Dinner Menus meets all the needs of every home cook. This new release tastefully combines nutrition, ease of preparation and cost-efficiency while offering not just single dish recipes but full meal menus—one for every day of the year! With homespun charm, warm wit and playful trivia, home-cooks are provided with a ready-made plan for entire meals that are fun, cheap and quick. *365 Quick, Easy and Inexpensive Dinner Menus* is a cookbook for the entire family and its innovative menus have been approved by kids nationwide. The book is multi-indexed: by food category and by preparation time.

THE SINGLE PARENT RESOURCE

BY BROOK NOEL WITH ART KLEIN $13.95
ISBN   1-891400-44-4

What kind of help do single parents need most in their day-to-day lives? The authors asked that question of over 500 single parents. Now they provide the answers to the top concerns, problems and challenges of single-parent life. Here they are—practical, concise, timely, relevant—and never before available in a single guide!

Getting Up, Getting Over, Getting On:
A Twelve Step Guide to Divorce Recovery

BY MICKI MCWADE $14.95
ISBN 1-891400-13-4

For 20 million Americans the long process of healing after the devastation of divorce began with a single step. Most found their way alone, making mistakes and trying to reinvent their lives through trial and error. Now, borrowing the wisdom gained in the development of 12 Step Programs, this new book offers learned and proven support. Author Micki McWade adapts the best techniques, information and life lessons of long established recovery programs to provide a concise and comprehensive pathway to a fulfilling life after divorce. Whether during the painful days of the divorce itself or in the adaptive weeks and months that follow, McWade offers valuable ideas that work in relationships with children, with in-laws, and with (ex) spouses. Readers are also provided with step-by-step encouragement for forming their own support groups.

TATIANA

BY GREG ANDERSON $22.95

What appears at first to be a simple accident soon becomes a web of deadly agendas when a young woman capture on videotape the horrific crash of an airliner into the deserted Dutch countryside. News accounts detail the final moments of Moscow Air 119, but when they're drastically different than what Tatiana's camera recorded, she fights to make her tape public and is immediately fighting for her very life. On the run in both Europe and North America, Tatiana finds herself trapped between three disparate governments. Unfooled by the mirage of protection, Tatiana plots her own way out as the deadly triangle closes in around her. When no place is safe, Tatiana turns to the one person she has always counted on...herself.

*Educational and Group Discounts are available
for more information write to CHAMPION PRESS, LTD.*

Please photocopy this page to order additional copies of Champion titles. Or order on-line at our web site, www.championpress.com.

QUANTITY	TITLE	PRICE EACH	TOTAL

	SHIPPING & HANDLING $3.95 for the first book and $1 more for each additional book		
		TOTAL	

☐ **Payment enclosed**

☐ **Please charge my** ☐ **VISA** ☐ **MASTERCARD**

    Account number _____ **expiration date** _____

    Signature _____

    Name as it appears on card _____

Name _____

Address _____

City _____ **State** _____ **Zip** _____

Day Phone _____

Autograph Copy ☐ **Yes** ☐ **No**

MAIL FORM TO:

**Champion Press, Ltd.
PMB 207
12919 NE Hwy 99th
Vancouver, WA 98686-2711**